Flowers Leaning Toward the Sun
by Ry Downey

This book is dedicated to Dustyn Hunt
October 1, 1997 - February 25, 2019
BLACK LIVES MATTER

The lines in quotations found in "End of an Era" are all taken from songs by Nirvana or quotes from Kurt Cobain himself.
Book Cover Art by Eli Klemmeck [@neomlei]
Book Cover Design by Ashleigh Darby

Find Ry Downey:
Instagram: @ryofwands
Facebook: www.facebook.com/ryduzpoemsgewd
Wordpress: www.wordpress.com/ryduzpoemsgewd

-author's note-

Hello, dear reader, and welcome to my book! Here you will find references to sex, drugs, infidelity, blasphemy, heresy, witchcraft, paganism, the occult, politics, and just a little bit of violence (hey I had to sell the book somehow). If any of these topics make you uncomfortable, please put this book down immediately (or keep reading).

I'd like to tell you a little bit about this book and how it came to be. After my most recent breakup, I moved back into the house in Seattle that I'd left in order to live with my girlfriend at the time. I also moved into the deepest depressive episode of my life. And one not so special day, a little voice spoke up in the back of my head. A very angry little voice. It spoke the words that would become my poem, "Nuclear Summer." I finished the poem and found that I actually liked it. I had tried to write poems before, but they always came off sounding like someone trying to write a poem. The kiss of death for anyone trying to write real poetry. I posted the poem on my social media account and got far more responses than I expected. So many that I eventually got the idea that maybe I should write more. And that's exactly what I did. Almost three years later and here is a book full of them.

This book is supposed to be the story of one person's spiritual, emotional, mental awakening. The book is split into three sections, each serving its own purpose. The poems will vary in voice and tone and technique. I have a feeling that the poems at the beginning of the book will speak to some more than the poems near the end and the other way around. Even poetry collections have endings and for good reason. I hope you find the reasons here. Thank you so much for putting yourself here. My never ending love goes to you. Thank you.

-ry

Flowers

-to the reader-

to you the reader:
this is my poem
where i speak
to you
and apologize
for the fact that it seems
like every time you read
one of these little ditties
i either end up complaining
or crying
or both.

i never liked the Confessionalists
when I was younger.
in poetry class they always seemed
like a bunch of pussies,
complaining and whining about
how hard their lives were--
my perspective has broadened
a bit. now I think that maybe
they were just people
having a hard time
who found their outlet through poetry.
i feel like i'm becoming one of them
because my life isn't as hard
as it seems. but it's all i can do
to keep from throwing in the towel.

i will also confess
that i'm too much of a pussy
to kill myself--
so please don't worry yourself over that.
this is just my chance to drop the act
that you and i both perform--
the one where you read the poem

as if it wasn't written for you,
it being instead a private look
into a feeling person's head,
like a diary or private thought
snatched from the ether--
and where i write a poem
for the sake of writing a poem,
like no one is ever going to read it,
just the artist's struggle to deal
with his own demons.
because obviously that's crap.
you're here reading
and i'm here writing,
us both knowing the other's
role in this act.
i'm sorry it seems like every poem
i write is full of sad shit--
but i'm also not going to stop.
the fact is that right now,
in this moment, i'm full of sad shit.
and this is the only place where i can
get it out. and right now
you may be thinking, "oh, don't be sorry."
but the fact is that i am.
i wish i could write a poem just as moving
about a cat
or snow falling past the halo
of the streetlights.
and if i read this in front of you,
you'd probably tell me not to say sorry.
but what do you think you'd get
in return?
another apology. so thank you
for listening to me ramble
here.

i hope one day i will get better
at changing how i feel

or writing poems that
someone
will call great.
but until that day,
thank you
and i'm sorry.

-my old bullshit-

I crave your hippie bullshit--
it used to be mine, too.
Magic, attraction, manifestation--
these used to be my mantras,
but no more.
Entropy, apathy, and self-
pity are my shit now.

Energy at an all time low.
I can't see beyond the rim
of this hole I've dug myself.
I'm the master of my own destiny,
I believe that too. No longer
interested in the result. I watch
my movements like I'm someone
else. I am no longer me,
ignorant of myself.
The solutions that come
to mind all just seem like too much
work. I know exactly what you'll say.
Instead I just sit
here in my bed,
typing these words,
a conversation with myself.
I'm the only one who will let me talk.

It might not be the best solution.
It's the only one I want.
I'm not the best person
to be giving myself advice--
but it's better that way
because I never take my own advice--
or anyone else's.

Stop being a depressed piece of shit
is my favorite mantra--
it does nothing to help me out.

My friend gave me a tarot reading
earlier today and it fucked me in the ass--
no lube. It said the same thing that I say
to myself--stop being a depressed piece
of shit--I guess that's the answer.
The truth is never fun to hear.

-kill your idols-

You raised the idea
of us running away
together. In that moment
I swear I saw us side
by side, unknowing
where we were going.
Headlights illuminating
just enough of the path.
We had faith to follow.

I scoffed at your suggestion.
Said something about
how far I've come.
I have a job now,
a place to live,
and a savings--a pile
of money I'm not
supposed to use.
What good does that do me?
I'm realizing that I'm scared
and lonely
and so tired of being
responsible
and alone.

I'm a free spirit.
Belonging
to the universe
with no one to call mine
and no one
to call me theirs
makes me think of Bukowski.
I admire that man
and hope that my words
are something like his

in how they slice your guts
open and at the same time
rub your back
and let you know
everything is going to be okay
even if it's not.

I hope to be like Bukowski,
but at the same time,
I don't. He died
alone and miserable
of cancer of the liver,
because he drank himself
into a place where the sharpness
of the world
was dull enough to bear.

I'm too much like him already.
Was he a hopeless romantic
who became ultimately
hopeless?
If I could spend time
with one famous person
from the past, it would be
him. I'd probably try to match
him, drink for drink,
and when I failed,
with my head hanging
heavy over a puddle
of sick, I would spit,
wipe my mouth,
straighten up, and ask:
"Did you ever believe in true love?"

I used to. Fuck, I used to
believe so hard. I was
a believer and that carried
me everywhere. Still romantic,

still hopeless, struggling
with believing in anything
anymore.

-i am blessed in all this mess-

I sit outside the RV
on the ground next to a pile
of my things
dropped on the lawn.
Books and posters,
a broken picture frame.

I'm so blessed
in all this mess,
falling
pieces and echoes
conjuring a maelstrom
of feelings
from every
direction,
shattered and staring
accusations writ in glass
seven years of bad luck
that will be spent unraveling
and dissecting
and separating
between
what was real
and what was fake
and what was both.

Wind picks up
my hair, sticks it
to my wet cheeks.
Trees surround me
and our old home
in the woods.
They dance
back and forth
to the music

of the wind.

I find who I am
and what I'm about
in the midst
of this mess
and broken glass
catching glimpses
of my higher self,
white puffy clouds
most certainly not
the cracks in the glass
I know soon
I will be stronger
in the broken
places.

The glue to unpuzzle
this puzzle doesn't exist
in matter.
Spirit is the only thing
completing the picture,
making me whole
so I will fuck and shit and goddamnit
and fuck you motherfucker, I see
you. Take a look at yourself and ask
if you're proud of what you've
done.

I repack the box slowly.
This is the last time
I will be here.
Walk my things
to the car,
put them in.
One last look,
a souvenir.
This will never break.

And I will do this with a smile
until I've purged myself
of that hair in my mouth
that eyelash in my eye
and since you are neither cold
nor hot
I will spew you
from my mouth
until I'm left knowing
I'll be fine.

-black skinny jeans-

My mom bought me these pants.
That's why they work so well--
they were bought with love.
They're black
and skinny
and they feel like a hug
from my mom.
I wear these pants
every
single
day.

I wear them to the club--
they're part of my uniform
for any
and every
occasion. I dance and dance
and dance and sweat
and most of the time
I don't wash them after.
They are now a part of me
just like my mom.

I wore them to my brother's wedding
along with a tie-dye shirt
where I made everybody
get up and dance--
and when I gave the speech
at the reception my mom begged me
to give while I was frying
on mushrooms. I remember
remembering
out loud a story of my brother
when we were young where he said,
"If I fall in love, I'm going to fall

hard." I wished the newlyweds
all the happiness in the world.
I remember my brother crying
and getting up to hug me.
We hadn't talked
in two years.

These pants are made for wearing
and that's what I do.
I can fall asleep in them
like they were pajama pants.
Many nights I've woken up
in a reminder
of my mother's love.
I had a pair just like them.
I wore a hole through
the ass. Now there's a Hocus Pocus
patch where the hole was--
I wear them on special occasions
when magic is needed.

My mom always asks me,
"Are you sure those aren't too tight?"
And I laugh and wear them
until they fit
just right.
I don't know if she knows
why I started wearing them
in the first place.

When I was still a teenager
I Googled "how to make yourself
look taller." The tip that stood
out most was, "wear slimmer pants--
it lengthens the legs
creating the illusion
of height."

Thank you, mom,
for helping
your shorter son
feel
as tall as he
felt
he needed to be.

-karma-

you hit me up today
to ask me to help heal
the wounds you made yourself.
you ask me if my karma
has been repaid
for the things i did--
and i say yes i believe
it has. you were the instrument
of my karma
and you are again, returning
here
to dredge up the past
and help me remember
how it was paid.

what if i said my biggest
regret wasn't you, but how
we were so perfect
at one point,
and how far it fell
before the end?

and now here you are again
asking if my sins will be repaid
when you've saved the universe
the trouble. i fucked up first
it's true, but what are my fuck ups
when compared with you?

-august 17 2016, seattle wa-

-anxiety-

i knew depression
was a paralytic,
but that was before
i felt anxiety.
don't
fucking
move.
self-check
every
single
second.
if you're not busy
you're fucked.
mind spinning
circles
with no center.
can't breathe
at all.
drink some water
try not to choke.

what the fuck
is wrong
with me?

no reason to feel
this way--
well except for the fact
that the world is pissed off
and trying to flick us
off its back.
this is what comes
when apathy
is trending.

can i not breathe
because i'm panicking
or because everything
around me
is burning?

i'm jealous of animals
and little insects
who only know how to do.
constantly on the move
or sleeping--
i'm too lazy for that.
uncomfortable all the time
because of my addiction
to comfort.

i need a change
but what kind?
what will kill this
constant
buzzing
in the back of my brain
that says i'm not doing enough?
self love
apparently
isn't enough anymore.
the healthier i get,
the more poisoned
my comfort.
what's the point of living
longer
when everything is a struggle?
i promised twenty seven more
years.
i promised
twenty seven
more
years.

i promised.

-sex isn't love-

It's been a year since I told you
to get out of my house.
Right before, you asked me
if we were friends anymore.
I had to say no.

I haven't seen you in a year.
How do I write a poem about you
and make it really
about me?

A glimpsed picture of her,
something inside me reaches
for mornings with legs entwined,
shared cigarettes,
depths of eyes that words
do less than sounds
and colors
can do to evoke.

It's necessary
in moments
like these
to conjure
the bad times.
Let them bluely battle
to bring to bear balance
slackening my grip.

Lies lied looking left
and right in my eyes.
Sitting in a car outside
a building in the rain,
phone pressed against ear,
no sound of voice but a tone

like a drone entering ear
reminding me that no response
is also a response.

This seems to be working.
I feel better already.
I already deleted the naked
pictures.

The experts say that's the hardest.

-miscarriage-

When we were younger,
once,
and in love,
we were making
love,
on acid.
Root chakras connected,
speaking words without
lips
tongues
teeth
or breath,
minds melding,
I remember
I thought to you
that if I were
to release
inside you,
that I would
raise
our child
and never leave.
You felt my release
coming. Eyes widened,
you jumped off me
quicker than I'd ever seen
you move. And my release
poured forth
onto me,
into nothing.
And right then
I felt what I'd never
imagined: the loss
of a child.
I remember crying

right then,
covering my face.
You came and comforted,
I remember that,
too. I'm sorry
I wasn't the one.
Neither were you.

-the poetry of it all-

I remember I was doing coke one night
at a friend of a friend's house.
We were there for a bit
and then I was told I couldn't stay there
anymore. That I'd have to find somewhere
else to go. I shrugged and said okay.
But, I was curious as to why.

He told me his housemate was Nick.
Then he said his last name.
I cast backward in my memory,
fishing for a connection.
Then I remembered.
Then I reacted...my eyes widened,
I felt disbelief spread across my face
and I started to laugh.

"Word," was all I managed to say.
I'd met Nick's girlfriend at a party
a year or so ago. Right around the time
my own relationship was falling apart.
(Oddly enough, *his name* was Nick, too.)
She and I talked and smoked on the balcony
of their house during a party in the summer.
We got to know one another. Her body was holy.
Her soul was so new.
We slept together
a few different times.
And then she told me she loved me.
I told her she was wrong.
"No," she said, "I know when I'm in love."

I didn't see her again.
And I still haven't. But we still talk
every now and then.

The attraction is still there
and I think maybe
even some love.

She asked me once before it was over
how I could be okay
with what we were doing.
I thought for a moment
before I replied and my own lover's face
swam before me.
I said that the amount of pleasure from this
outweighed my guilt because it was the closest thing
to forgetting my pain.
I feel like maybe we could have been together.
But the timing wasn't right. Like me having to leave
my buddy's house because of my past
betrayal. I had to find somewhere else to go
and I still laughed because of the poetry
of it all.

It was okay, though. I had my car
and lived like a mile away.
I had somewhere I could go.

-untitled-

I just wrote a poem
about sleeping with a taken woman
after I'd just been cheated on.
I sit here and I wonder on why
it is that writer's destroy so much.
Are we so starved and desperate
for stories we will break anything:
hearts, promises, bottles, windows,
just to have something
to put in ink on that blank sheet--
the one thing we know will never
leave?

-so over you-

Is it wrong to say I hate
loving you if I don't say it
in person?
Because I'd never do that,
you know--I'm far too kind
and cowardly. I suppose
I would call it that.
I can't help but smile
at the sight of you
and hug you
longer than I should,
even though you've told me
more than once
to come pick up my shit
from the place we used to share.
These things are hard to feel,
harder to say--
I love myself
but I love you more,
and I hate loving you
more. In glimmering glimpses
my heart lives outside
my chest. Frostbitten,
now I put it back in.
There will be no reunion.
By now I'm not sure I'd want it.
It's buried under the things
you didn't tell me
and what I'm left to wonder.
You say you're too crazy.
Tell me how love exists without that.
We're all fucking crazy--
especially when it comes to love.
Not only are we crazy.
We're also dumb as fuck.

I'm so over you
I'm buried beneath your feet,
breathing in the acrid odor
of our love gone to seed,
buried before its time.

-room to breathe-

The house is quiet now that he's gone.
He wanted to move out,
said he didn't want to pay the rent
anymore.

So he went backward to his dad's house
to live easier. Whatever that means.
But they are engaged.
So now what? She wonders.

The house is quiet now without his noises--
playing games on the computer,
random bursts of speech from him to his friends
online or to her.

Maybe she'll get into a new routine--
yoga every morning and maybe
exercise. Anything to avoid falling back
toward rock bottom.

The house is quiet now. It doesn't feel like peace
and quiet. It just feels like quiet. And maybe death.
She knows there are ghosts in the house. She's seen them
move things and slam doors shut.

It feels like she's losing weight
She doesn't have a scale or anything.
She feels good in her body
and that's something.

Nothing left to focus on but here. But now.
She takes a breath and lets it out,
looks around the room. At least his stuff is gone now.
More room to breathe.

-advice from a 21st century American failure-

When you are born
try to come out
screaming. It will
announce your presence
to the world
and spare you the indignity
of being slapped on the ass.

When you are young,
experience all the world
has to offer
before they put that
fucking screen
in front of your face.

Express gratitude
and love
for your parents.
They are the only
ones who will love
you no matter what,
and not everyone
is able to experience
that.

When you're in school,
get good at talking
with people. That skill
will pay off far better than any
GPA. Also make sure to do
your work. School is pointless
and brainwashing, but
it's too fucking easy
to not even pass.
And you'll need those grade

points when it comes time
to apply for college.

Don't go to college
unless you're sure
you're either going to get grants
or make enough money
to pay back your loans.
Or if you have really rich
parents. But if you do,
don't take the major
they tell you to.

If you take out loans,
you're fucked,
so resign yourself
to lifelong debt.
and shitty credit
that will fuck you up
for life.

When you get a job
make sure you go
to bed early enough
to get good sleep
so you don't rest
through your alarm
enough times
to get fired.

And before you go to sleep,
be sure you brush
and floss your teeth
so you don't have half
your teeth filled
with metal by the time
you're thirty.
Teeth like that

won't stand up long
when we have no dentists
after whatever apocalypse
finally comes.

And lastly,
treat everyone
like they're your brother
or sister,
because let's face it,
they pretty much are.
And at some point
we will all be at the mercy
of someone
or something,
be it fellow human being,
animal
or the hand of fate.

-hunter s thompson blues-

i'm so sick of being
the way i am.
nothing is ever good
enough for me.
the desire to improve
comes and goes. motivation
fades and appears
the way the strobe
of a lighthouse
appears
and vanishes.
one friend says I'm stagnant.
another says I'm improving.
i don't know who to believe.
i push away those
who would love
me and content
myself with the life
of a hedonist.
i'm not too concerned
with finding someone
to love
because I avoid it
without even thinking.
i attract people who
use me
and my kindness
until nothing is left
and i'm left
where i was
before.
i guess that explains
my situation
but i'm still at odds
as to how to change.

i had an idle
thought about suicide
today
at the happiest place
on earth.
almost 30.
already tired.
i committed
to living til
fifty four
and I'm already
regretting it.

-august, salmo river ranch, b.c.-

-epitaph-

I'm in love with someone
who might not love me back.
It's not as bad
as it sounds.
Or maybe it is.
My feelings on the matter run
back and forth
between
feeling pathetic and unloveable
to
immense heights of ecstasy.

The latter comes after
minor things
like when she looks me in the eyes
and smiles
while I'm driving
or when she reaches over
and takes my hand.
Such bliss is unparalleled
for me.

The former come in the dead
of night
when I'm tired and emotions
are far harder to control--
messages unanswered,
pictures I view on my phone
of that fuck
wearing the necklace she gave
me when she was in love
with both of us.

My friends tell me I should just leave
her alone. Cut off contact

and save myself. Self love
is what they call it
and they might be right.
But what if I love myself
too much to not
know who I want
and go after her?

That line from the movie
I suggested we watch
together--
"Don't ever let anyone
ever tell you you can't
have something you
really
want.
Go for it." It definitely applies
here.
Imagine a headline
or an epitaph--
or a line on a headstone--
"MAN LIVES REST OF LIFE IN LOVE
WITH ONE PERSON
AND THEY
WERE NEVER
TOGETHER--
SAVE ONE MONTH."
Does that make you sad?
How would you think
of that man?
Why do I ask
if I don't care?
I used to ask the opinion
of friends
on this matter.
But not anymore.
You're not my friend
or maybe you are--

I don't really care
what you'd think
or how you'd feel.
I just want to ask the question--
because it makes me wonder
what I'd think
if that man turned out to be me.

I only expect to live another twenty-six
years. And I've been in love
in some fashion
a few times already.
Do you want to know the real
number?
Five.
The number is five.

I'm done with being in love
again.

-killin it-

My homie said, "Kill it."
So I did.

They say these things will kill me.
Maybe that's what I'm banking
on. I always joke and say
the day I don't want to die,
not even a little,
is the day I'll quit.

I took the last drag
of the cigarette, turning
it into a butt.
A butt is a corpse.

My dad's dad
was a smoker.
Packs on packs
on packs.
A piece of his lung
ended up removed.
Then he switched to Pepsi.
His teeth ended up rotten.
He ended his life
wearing dentures.
Substitutes do no good.
All or nothing
is the name of the game.

I watched the last breath
of the thing float away.
Blue steely scented smoke
wafted away from my lips.

My parents ran marathons

and never smoked once.
I used to run, too--
lungs pink as a sunrise.
After I quit smoking weed
because it drove me nuts,
I started smoking cigs.
More substitutes,
less progress. Then why
does it feel so good?

It was comforting to know
that even as it drifted
away from its body,
I could still see it for a time--
and even after it was gone
I knew it remained.

-independence day, 1999-

I must confess I don't remember
most of my Independence days.

But there is one
that does stand out.
My mother father brother
and I came to a family
member's house—I don't remember
which—but I think it was near
George, Washington. How appropriate!

Everyone was getting drunk
or was already drunk.
It seems my family has a problem
with alcohol. Clinking of bottles
and hillbilly laughter—my family
are all cowboys, you see.
And so was I
until I got older.

Country music played and bugs buzzed
in the itchy dry grass that sprouted
and asked without words
for water. Does anyone else feel
this sense of awkwardness
around his family? Not sure what to say.
No, please, Aunt Jill, don't kiss me.
I don't want it. That was every time
I saw her.

I was here and I had been here before
but I'd never wanted to be.
Interactions forced by the ties that bind--
blood is the worst because it breeds
obligation. I didn't know these people

and still don't. They are a part of me
that still goes untapped
every year. The more I know myself
the more I know
I am not them.

It finally got dark, the fireworks started.
I don't remember anything with my family
here, now. I sat on the itchy blanket
in the itchy grass. But the booms
from the bursts of light blasted
through me and knocked knowledge
of me and mine and ours far away
from where I sat. I no longer felt
my legs or their itch.

Spectacle of sparks and sun and starbursts
spread their fingers from the centerpoint
of the color concussion and shook me
to the core. I remember sitting cross
legged with my mouth open.
A lawn chair exists in my memory
on my periphery, just barely visible.
I am sitting in it.

-secret-

I've always been a secret
for you.
No trace of me
on the performance art
of your profiles--
these seem like paltry
things to put into a poem
but it's the language
you and our friends
seem to understand.

I miss that friend of yours
who was with us that night
at the bus stop
where we waited
for her bus with her.
You told me
after I went back to the house
to do a thing,
she turned to you
and she said,
"That boy, he really
loves you."
And you told her "I know."
Where has that friend gone?
Do you still know?

Do you care to let anyone
who knows you
see the love I hold
for you?
I keep all this space
around me clear
from others who would love me
for you.

Are these labors of love lost
on you?
In every gesture of flowers
and late night food runs,
all I seem to get is a form letter
"Thanks" and hours upon hours
of silence.

I've never met someone so annoyed
by love. Why does affection scare you?
You don't say it
but that's always worse--
if you said that you didn't care
about me, it would be a lot easier
than you showing it--
I'm a verbal person
and lack of communication
seems to be kind of your thing.

I say, "I love you."
You say, "Olive juice."
What the fuck does that
mean? Tomatoes and potatoes
both splattering the walls
I painted tie dye for you--
the only color of love.
Green is a starting place,
but rainbows are really my thing.
You make my colors run
until they all turn
a different shade
of brown.

I fear I've gotten off the topic--
the point of it is,
no one knows about me
but they know about her
and him--

the worst part is
you know exactly who I mean.
I'm just a mistake,
an accident you made
that you're too scared to accept
or let go.
I don't know how much longer
I'll be here--I know I told you
I'd be here waiting,
but it's hurting my hands
to hold the rope,
and I'll let you in on something else,
something someone told me
a while back--
friends don't make secrets
and secrets don't make friends.

I still remember
when you said
our child would be
beautiful.

-truth, no chaser-

I have to remember for next
time that when someone
says, "I don't want a relationship"
I should always tack on
"...with you" to the end.
Experience lends another
lesson.

I'm obviously not as woke
as I'd like to think if I'm begrudging
you the happiness you seem
to have found, the same sort
I sought to find with you.
It's not unconditional
love if this is where I draw
the line.

Do we really think we're doing good
when we aim to save people
from being hurt? You told half
of the truth and saved
your conscience from the bruise
of seeing my face
when I realized.
You weren't around to hear
the tree fall. It did make a sound.

These little shards of truth
will never add up
to more than a lie.
The pain that we save
each other from
is nothing more
than how we hide
ourselves from the damage we do.

I want to be as woke
as I think I am.
I'm no different
than anyone else.
It's why I said "we"
in this poem about you
and how much I hurt
from the pain
you saved me from.

You taught me another
lesson: when I say "you"
I also mean "me."
We are reflections
of each other—we
said that the first time
we hung out and hiked
into the woods.

Please save me no more--
and I'll do the same for you.
We are adults and take
care of ourselves. All I ask
from you is truth,
no chaser. I'm a big boy
and you're a big girl.
It's time to grow up.

-trash day-

last week was my week
to take out the trash.
i did it without
complaint, expecting
the next person to follow suit.
expectations rarely align
with reality--the trash piles up,
not responding to my wishes,
or to my dreams.

i'm still trying
to keep from being sad
about you throwing me out--
it makes me project
how the trash feels
sitting in its bin
that now sits on the curb,
because i took it out myself.

i hope you don't do the same things
with him that you did with me--
i hope he doesn't pull your hair
or push your buttons
the way i did
when i wanted to troll you
just because i knew you'd smile.
does he make you think
about outer space, or
why we dream what we dream?
did he ever talk about your parents
hurting you, or what kind of flowers
you want at your wedding?

i feel like i could have done better
but also that i didn't do that bad.

what do i say to my friends
when they ask me what happened--
how weak does it sound
when i can't say that we grew apart
or that we agreed it was for the best,
but rather that one day you just decided
that you'd grown tired of me?

and then you told me to leave,
that i should move up north.
where does the trash go
when it's asked to leave?
you didn't take me out,
but i'm quite considerate.
i took myself out instead.

i'm sitting here in the landfill,
part of a rejected cast
of characters, living in a house
full of man children, adults
who never learned how to adult.
i feel like you should be here too--
that was the plan after all,
but who am i to complain
about being set free?

-bait and switch-

I've been told
if someone is on your mind
you're on theirs too.
God I hope it's true
because you're running
ruts into my brain--
it was sunny today but it felt like rain.

I told myself I wasn't
going to message you first
but I see you online and what
do I do? You already know
because I'm here
waiting on a reply from you
again.

Everything I've ever let go
has claw marks on it.
I don't want to let go of you
because you've been marked up
enough--I want to be the one
who makes you brand new,
a new beginning.

I hope you're happy with where
you are, because I'm sure as hell
not. At least it wouldn't be a total
waste, this feeling like a middle finger
from a stranger. Equivalent exchange
is the phrase that comes to mind:
please be in heaven while I'm in hell.

Because if we're in this together
we might as well be together.
Does that make sense? I hope

it does because my life has felt
like a waste until I met you.
Now I'm wasting more time waiting
for you to tell me you're ready.

Why can't I quit you? What the fuck
did you do to deserve me?
All this devotion for someone
who sold me love and a pretty
face, then stopped selling
when she realized she had me
hook, line, and sinker.

I'm definitely hooked
and as a matter of fact,
I'm a landed catch--
a salmon if you will,
rainbow colored and
iridescent, gasping for water
to filter through and deliver me
breath.

-up in flames-

When I was nine I learned about
spontaneous combustion.
It became my new favorite
fear. Thoughts of erupting
into flames, blisters bursting
on my skin, becoming a fireball
kept me up at night. Now I think
it's the only way I should die.

An endless sun burns
somewhere inside, and it feels impossible
that it will ever fizzle out--
rather it should sink and then explode
into overwhelming supernova.
A rushing and boiling of blood
and brain chemicals erupting
into torn flesh and viscera
painting everything red,
a galaxy of guts.

I can't be contained, even though
I've tried. I remember a friend saying
to me once: "I love you man,
but sometimes you're a little bit
much." I've heard this in different
words from different mouths.
So much so that now it's down
as fact in this poem.

The closest I ever get to feeling
complete is when I'm at a show
and I lose myself within the body
of the beat, adrift but found,
turned on and tuned in, out
of body experiencing the thing

that tells me I'm not alone. A slave
to the groove, air collapses in my lungs
and a rushing in my ears swells
my heart until I'm on the verge
of bursting into flames...

or when I'm making the beast
with two backs with someone
as crazy as me. We rock
to the rhythm and she cries
out, saying some crazy shit,
calls me "Daddy" and leaves
bloody trails down my back
and I feel myself erupting
somewhere below.

And then I'm back in this body
cursed with this brain
that can't deal with its problems,
pushing them into the back
of the brain until it breaks
the surface of the pensive
placid waters of the psyche
and I can't even drink a glass
of water without choking
on the reality that everything
is burning. I smell it in my nostrils
all the time and sometimes I think
that I'm the one burning.

I have a handful of goddesses
who I'm half in love with
and the half could be whole
with a single word.
But they all want to belong
to the universe and not
my ass. They've seen too much
of this hot mess

to even come close enough
to feel the warmth
that comes from the source.

We came from the earth--
I came from the earth--
and part of me burns
every time the trees
catch on fire. And before
that we came from the stars.
I am stardust, I am earth,
and one day our sun will
die--and my first genesis
will swallow my second,
and on that day my destiny
will be fulfilled.

-sanger-

I'm so fucking angry
all the time.
Why does everyone
piss me off?

You ever see that meme
where the guy is wearing
a mask that says "angry"
and someone asks him
why he's so angry all the time?
And he lifts the mask
and underneath it says
"Sadness." The guy says, "Let's
just put that back." And
he replaces
the mask.

Maybe it's kind of like that.
I definitely recognize
that beneath all the clubs
and friends and my job
I'm still sad. But no one
likes to look at that.
I get hit up far more
when I'm angry
than when I'm down.

Maybe everyone is like this,
and that's why everyone
is mad. Are we all just incredibly
sad? I wish I had the answers
to all my questions. But shit
in one hand and wish in the other
and see which fills first.

I feel like the main difference

between

anger and sadness
is that one is
seen as productive

and the other

is a paralytic.

Tell your friends you're mad
and they will ask why
and when you tell them
they will at least have something to say.
Tell your friends you're sad
and they will ask you why
and by the time you're done explaining
they'll already be wanting to dip.

It's almost like you caught
something
and everyone is super down
with not catching
what you have.

My friends tell me I care
too much
and let people put their shit
on me.
I guess it's the only way I've
found
to keep the friends I have.

-am i ugly yet?-

Abandon your loved ones.
The ship is sinking--
women and children last--
me first.
Me. Me. Me.
Everyone fucking look at me.
100 likes on this new post--
I'm so happy.
Yeah. Yell at me
for throwing my cigarette
out my car window.
We're bulldozing the Amazon
to raise the cows
in your cheeseburger
you probably ate
earlier today.
Your road rage screams
the evidence
that we are apes
with ego trips
driving two-ton
vehicles.
There was this girl
and I don't call her
a woman
for this reason:
We fell in love
and she fell out of it,
and then she bled me dry
of nearly everything
I had to give.
And I know its no excuse
that it's helped me be
who I am now.
It's past 3am

and I'm high
on coke--
all the regular people
who I usually talk to
have gone to bed
and I'm horny.
Cycle through
the same three apps,
to find a cute girl
who's willing to let me
poke her.
I don't want you
to like my poems
or the person writing
them...I'm trying to paint
a picture--stand still--
of the two-toned nature
of all our existences
and the way we look
away
from all our own
atrocities
while we string others up
for theirs.

-don't ask me why I have no hope-

because if you do, i'll probably
say something like this:

if i end up having children,
they will most likely be the same
age i am today when it's confirmed
that all ocean life is extinct,
essentially signaling the end
of human life on Earth.

it's getting to the point
where having children is no longer
a financial issue,
but a moral one.
i ask myself about the ethics
of whether or not i want
my child to inherit this Earth.

the money hoarders
and plan schemers
and the inheritors of small
million dollar loans
are tightening the noose.
whatever power we have
drips away with each shrug
of our shoulders.

i cry at least once
every single day.
i care about so much
it feels like suffocating.
my mind is on fire at every
moment i'm awake. sleep
is a godsend, a way to dull
the roar that tears a hole

in every waking moment.
anxiety is as constant
as the beating of my heart.

i never believed in God
but now i can't stop
praying, asking him to save
us all. "they know not
what they do," is a common
refrain.

the best hope we have
is those who aren't even old
enough to cast their votes.
they are the ones taking
the capital to court. it's theirs
and our future together
that is punctuated
with a question mark.

i have a housemate
who says that recycling
doesn't even matter.
doesn't.
even.
matter.
it's been a long time
since i literally saw
red.

in these moments
i'd like to not be held
responsible for what i say.
i want an apology.
i want. a fucking. apology
from those who have the power
to do something
but don't.

i imagine their apologies
sometimes
when i want to feel better.
they are on their knees,
preferably crying,
hands clasped in a plea
for mercy, forgiveness,
redemption.

i'd like to see them strung
up. lifeless. corpses
to feed the same birds
that die
with soda can tabs, trash bags,
and used condoms
in their bellies.

i'm not as woke as you think
i am. there is a real
smoldering vengeance
inside this person. apathy,
a disease we have grown
within ourselves,
may be the final plague.

i imagine my own apology--
something
very much like that--
to my own children,
if i were to have them.
"I'm sorry. I'm so sorry.
Forgive me. Please forgive
me."

-growing up-

I remember growing up.
The more time passed,
the fewer friends my parents
seemed to have.
I remember asking myself,
"Is this what growing up is?"
I wanted no part of it then.
Nothing much has changed.

It's getting harder and harder
to accept the fact that I'm
growing up. And if I'm not,
then everyone around me
seems to be. The people
I used to see every week
hardly come around.

Everyone is pairing off,
cuffing themselves
to a perceived fountain
of happiness. And I get tired
of picking up the pieces
and restarting from where
we left off.

I know distance is an illusion
And if I want to look
for those I love,
I need nothing more
than to close my eyes
and look within. But
that doesn't help me here
and now when loneliness
bends its fingers around
the door frame.

We are never alone
but that doesn't stop
the thoughts of how lonely
I am. I amuse myself
with my phone and books
on my shelf, even a now
and then trip to the park--
but birds can't talk back
and the dogs walking around
have owners of their own,
leashes linking them together.

I'm getting itchy feet.
If lonely here, why
not lonely somewhere else?
My friends are all seeking
their fortunes where they
are drawn. Am I doing the same?
And if I am are they feeling
the same as me?
And if I'm not, why not?
I read *The Alchemist*
so why am I so attached?

Buddha said the root
of suffering is attachment.
I feel like this might hold the key.
I hold on to what I have
because nothing is guaranteed.
It could all be gone
in the snap of a neck.

Trying to find a way
to make sense of what
is right. Do I have a right
to feel the way I do? And
I hate the fact

that my life philosophy is playing
out right now. No right,
no wrong. It just is. What we
notice, we manifest.
I can't help but notice
everyone goes where
they want.

-a moment-

Allow me to indulge
my ego
for a moment.

I'd like to be known
as a prophet.
Someone who speaks
for the people
who don't have the words
and for the gods
who don't have a voice.

The ego is not evil
no matter what they say.
The key is to refuse
to be its slave. Without your sense
of self there is no growth
there is no awareness.
Do not forget
who you are
in order to fulfill
someone else's version
of what it is to be divine.

I thank my father
for giving me my ability
to listen. Through my stillness
I hear the word of God
ringing
from all corners
of the world.
Gratitude sharpens the flavor
of our blessings.
They grow in number
as appreciation swells.

Bless the friends who serve
as the prophet's
prophet. Even the inspired
need reminders.
We are all disciples
of some language
of truth—though the Tower
may be shattered,
we are united
in our recognition
of each other.

Bob Dylan was another prophet
who talked about being
someone else
from day
to day.
Nothing ever felt
more real
to me
than that phrase.
Identity is so fragile,
so why worry
about ego?
As much as we'd like to deny,
we all know what's best
for us. The problem
not being knowledge,
but its rejection.

Have we always had this problem
where we all know
so little
while thinking we know it all?
Did anyone listen
to thinkers
of the past,

or were they just written
off as lunatics
and madmen,
outliers
unfit to dwell
among others?
I guess it would make sense.
No one likes being called
out on their shit.

I won't tell you how
to live, but I will
show you what I see.
And if you are within
the scope
of my sight
you may be called out
for the things you do.
Please don't worry, though,
because I scrutinize
everyone,
the person writing this
the most.

-release-

I came here
to this sacred
place to bury
you and all
the things I felt
for you.

When I arrived
I realized that a burial
wasn't good enough
and it would only poison
the ground I found
so hallowed. I listened
to the music that once
was ours and I squeezed
the last waters from my
eyes and when I was finished
I set the memory of you
aflame, like the forest
burning in the distance,
and as you burned
I felt released
from the prison
I'd built for my heart.

I know I told you
those sounds and words
would always be ours
but for once I'm glad
to find that I was lying
about that. You will
probably always remember
me saying that, and will
always see my face
and hurt with a phantom

pain each time they greet
your ears, but I know
I won't. I've reclaimed
it all in the name
of my sanity.

I hate to admit
it gives me great
pleasure to think
my face will grace
your mind each time you
hear these songs,
and you will burn
with regret to know
you let me slip
away. I may be cruel
for this, but you ran
me through worse--
and besides, I never
said I was a saint.
Just another thing
for me to work on,
and I will try to replace
my wrath
with love,
and wash away
this stain
on my soul,
the way that the rains
came and put out
the raging fire
just miles away.

-august 14 2017, salmo river ranch, b.c.-

Leaning Toward

-nuclear summer-

i sit huddled in my bunker
while the news shouts at me
from upstairs
in the form of my housemate
who truly believes
that we need laws
in order
to live.
i can govern myself
quite easily.
how about you?

it's been almost three weeks
since we called it quits.
i've moved out
and back into the place
where it all began.
i was living upstairs then
now i'm in the basement.
i don't know if it means anything
or not.
all i know is i can see us
running from death
when we're the chicken
with its head cut off.

i don't need to read the news
to know what's going on.
more wars, more death, more money...
and now a commercial break:
buy shit
to fill the hole
that is your fear of dying.

i see my world

crumbling,
and in its struggle to maintain,
my loves are trying to fuck
and feel
their way
out of death.
and i'm sorry.

buy the big shiny car
to get the hot
plastic pussy
marketed to us,
free of hair
and other things
unfit to share.
keep the machine oiled
and ready to consume
us all
once we're free
of the womb.

i wish i was different.
my friends are fucking friends
of friends
to achieve their own
ends. and i feel
like i'm melting
under the heat of my shame.
i'm in the same boat,
selfish and
vain. so i sit in my room,
the basement where it's nice
and cool, and i castigate
myself with the weapon
of my words, wagging
a finger at you and me,
begging us to get better.

there's nothing but bad vibes
on the tv.
fear versus hate
being sold to us from every talking
head. and they pretend
that they don't see
just like my friends and me--
we're both blind in our own ways.
whatever it takes is what i'm saying,
and the oompa loompa and
two-face are duking
it out over a house
made by slaves.

i pray to god,
i pray to allah--
i pray to the thousand eyes
of the hindu gods,
to deliver my loves from this
crucible of shit--
my only fear
asks what shape such an almighty
flame might take--
whether nukes,
or fire,
or dinosaur's bane--
our sins may be the pins
in the grenade
of our fate.

-eviction notice-

The world is on fire.
Summer is here
and it's not treating
us well.
Seattle looks like LA
but it's not smog.
All the same
we did this to ourselves.

Back in high school
summer happened
to be nice
and cool
once.
Endless quips of,
"How bout that global warming?"
Hur hur hur...

How about now ?
They even changed the name:
now its climate change
and this shit is real.
100 today in the sun
in Seattle.
115 in Portland yesterday
and to the north,
shit is literally on fire.

We're the most evolved species,
that's what they say.
But it seems like we evolved
backwards to me. The conditions
of this planet
granted us what we have.
And then at some point,

many years ago,
some devils decided
that man must pay
to walk the earth.

Now we are repaying
the mother
by sticking her
in the sides
with shovels and axes
and offshore drills
And in return,
she may be readying
to flick us all off her back.

I feel anxious
every day.
Sometimes I think its the drugs,
other times I feel like I'm tapping
into the collective dis-ease
of every soul
walking the planet.
I'm done with money
and institutions
and paying rent
and being denied
a place to live
because my credit is poor.

I say we tear it all down
to the ground.
New paradigms
come with new modes
of thinking. No more
subjugation and obligations.
The land should be free
and we as well to walk
and work and reap the benefits

of the seeds we sow.

Get thee behind me, Moloch,
I will co-sign no more
to being a steward
of destruction.

-to my friends-

When I was younger
I was always the friend
who was left behind --
the one other friends
would hang up on
and make the butt
of their jokes.
I made best friends
and they moved
away with their families.
Maybe this is why I vowed
and learned to make myself
indispensable. Probably one
of my greatest magic tricks,
going from that to this--
life of the party and light
of so many people's lives.
But you should know
you're the light of mine,
too. I miss you so much
sometimes that it hurts.
I know distance is an illusion
but loneliness can strike
at any time and I remember
that we are all out here seeking
our own fortunes. We hang
out with each other
less and less. Instead
of grieving I choose to believe
it's a sign of us growing
into our personal power.
We all used to need
each other so much.
and now here we are, shedding
skins and evolving into ourselves.

Our reach extends beyond
presence, the circle holds
as it diminishes. This must
be growing up. I'm proud
of us, I really am. But sometimes
I still feel the hole cut
in the place where you
used to be.

-evolution-

I want to love people
but they make it so hard.
In meditation
it comes so easily,
or when listening
to medicine music.
All is well and we are all
reflections of each other.
Until I step outside.
There are people
who honk at old ladies
crossing the street.
People who smash their beer
bottles on the ground.
It's so hard to show
others what is sacred.
I've heard it said,
in order to make something
sacred, you name it as sacred
and then treat it as such.
Such an easy recipe.
Why then do I flick
my cigarette out the window?
Maybe we are reflections
of each other.
I strive to be a better
human. Sometimes
avoiding being human
is the best I can do.
Do you ever sit with your friends
and listen to music
and start dancing around
like a band of gorillas?
If not, you should try it
sometime. Make noises,

huff and puff and beat
your chest. Or maybe fling
your crap at the next passing
car. We are slightly more evolved
apes, driving two-ton machines.
Never forget this. It will bring
you good fortune. Also remember
good fortune for us
may not be the same for others.

-nucleus-

The night is cold
but I don't feel it.
It's out there.
We are here.
It slaps at my window,
pinprick patters of wet against glass.
You're here with me
in our nest
under blankets,
in my bed.
The sleeping bag serving
for my top blanket
is all the way unzipped,
my defenses
when I look into you.

The world outside is always
winter--no one knows it
like me and you--
but here tonight
pressed against your skin
I feel the warmth still within
us both--the warm little center
of the universe. We hold it
together. Four hands, one light.

Have you ever seen a flower
reaching toward the sun?
Our arms reach around
and hold us
like the cotton crib of infancy.
We bow into this touch,
and fingers feel their way
through hair, cueing closed lids
and secret purrs never heard.

Winter was never my time of year--
I sided with the bear,
sleeping my way through it.
How perfect then, that I should find you here--
when only cold rays of light would shine
and only skeletons of trees remain,
that you would appear to make "my"
into "our" and bring the sun
I thought was lost.

Endless sun glows from inside.
The stoniest parts of me
now flower and bud,
lotus from the mud..
How weird and how strange,
and lovely--I'd never known
how it worked
until we found us.

-blue is the heaviest color-

I fell in love with you
again today--
I really didn't mean to
and I hope you don't mind
but I'm beginning to see
that there are many layers
to this lovely sea.

I thought I was safe
sitting on the porch,
watching you standing there,
with the blue and the braid
in your hair, beads intertwined
like your fingers around
your cigarette.
You were wearing my
flannel shirt, with the gold
and the blue, and my spirit
hood like a scarf. In my things,
but completely yourself.

All I see is blue
da ba dee
da ba die--
that song seems so sad
but that movie we watched
together was right--
blue is the warmest color
and I feel it,
your color,
seeping deeper into me.

I saw you dancing to your sounds
pumping from the phone,
lost inside yourself

and I witnessed another moment
of your becoming.
It happened again--
I found another depth
to dive to, under the waves
of your being.

I'm sorry to lay this on you--
it seems so heavy
like the weight of infinite
fathoms of the ocean.
I know that you are healing
and are needing time
for your broken parts to mend.
But the weight of the water
only acts on the shell
that holds the piece of us
that loves.
Your spirit is not the shell
that feels the weight of
your hurt--your spirit
is the thing that will make you
stronger in the broken places.

You saw me see you
like you always do--
I was in the middle
of my next dive,
falling deeper into the blue--
the weight of my dive
welled up inside
until I felt tears swimming
on the brims of my eyes.
But instead of cry
I stared at you through
the veil of my tears
and you stood there
swimming, like a mirage

but better,
because you were real.

You might ask me how
the broken places will mend.
The break in the water
from a thrown stone
is eventually repaired
after the ripples have faded.
If time is like water,
with its ebbs and flows,
then the ripples are the
tickings of the clock,
risen and setting suns.
Ripples are the stitches
making the water
whole again.

I saw you
through my watery veil.
You were smiling
and your head was tilted to one side.
I told you I love you
and you giggled,
a sound much like a ripple,
then said, "But I'm not doing anything."
To which I replied
that you were just being--
that I love the way you are.

More laughter, more ripples--
more breaks in the water
healed. You said, "Now
that I know what it means
to be dead, I can start
living again." Your newness,
your becoming is the
sign that time is doing

its work. Have faith in it
like the promise that
the weight of the water
will carry you home.

-home-

I've finally come home
again. A place and time
where everyone is my
friend, and everyone
is beautiful
and recognizes
the beauty
of all. Here
we are truly
reflections
of each other.

The world divides
us, and we allow
it to happen.
It preys on the ego
and its mechanisms--
both to focus
on the negative
and to push itself
above others.

My first home
was with my family,
related by blood.
Though we are different,
we are also the same.
Why can't it be
the same with those
who appear so different?

-wubbalubadubdub-

my friends say i have a smile
you can see across the room
in the dark.
i smile even bigger
and dance around the room.
i'm the center of attention,
it's true-- the life
of the party
though no one has a clue
i'm putting on an act
only bo burnham could
see through.
so I yell "Wubbalubadubdub"
and everyone laughs--
when it's pretty clear if you watch the show
i'm dying here
really fucking slow.

i'll smile when i see you
and give you a great big
hug, tell you i love you
and tell you life is beautiful
when we're both on drugs.
but sometimes
the truth is i know
honey works better than vinegar
in attracting friends.
so i elect not to tell you what i think
in exchange for something
bright--i don't know what you'd call
real, but i can tell you this:
it's not only women who
say what they don't mean
and mean what they don't say.

the truth is i'm both sides at once--
i'm a tie-dye wearing
broken hearted loser.
and that's okay.
who is to say which one is more real--
the me who thinks the world
is beautiful,
or the one who thinks existence
is pain? true gemini showing through.

the fact is
i have more friends
now that i smile and look
on the bright side
than i would have if i wore black
every day and listened to sad
songs about how i found
a job and how heaven knows
i'm miserable now. i am fake,
fake if you say,
i don't care--
because i'm more loved
saying what i sometimes mean.

-cutting the cord-

The scene in *One Flew Over
the Cuckoo's Nest*
where MacMurphy yells,
"Get off of me!"
sends me into myself
and somewhere inside,
the hole I've cut
for others stings
and reminds me
of my sacrifice
for love.

I've been Papa
for so long.
It's become
its own habit.
I give and I give
not expecting
a return.
The well
is running dry. I've cut
so many slices
from myself
and served them out.
Now I've got a hole
that leaks as soon
as I refill.

I carry crosses,
burdens,
weight,
secrets,
debts,
and love
never mine

to bear. I was never
put here to make your life
easier. My life has become
an obligation
to serve whoever is next
in line to put their hand out,
asking for things
I have driven myself
to earn. Discipline
comes from within
and a majority
of the time,
that's what it takes
to be able to give
and build
and take for yourself.

I give what I've earned
because it's how
I show
love.
After giving
so much, I say
I've earned the right
to say "No"...to give
what I have never learned
to lend to myself.
I always choose
to let others cut
and I push myself
to the back of the line.

No more cutsies,
no more guilt.

I'm tired
and my shoulders ache.
The favor shop

is closing.
Come take what you can
before it's shut.
This sounds selfish
and I'm past caring.
Living for yourself
is not synonymous
with selfishness.
After all, how do you take
care of others
when those efforts
wither your roots?
It doesn't matter
how you feel...
your own oxygen
comes first.
I have to water myself
with the same love
I've shown to you.

-time wounds all heels-

I stayed awake last night
to see the sun
in a different way,
on the other side
of the day.
I'm tired of frowning
at the light
pouring through my shades.
Much more welcome
when it crowns by inches,
as if by my command.
I sit and watch its birth.
Patience is a virtue
a sunrise its reward.
A twin of waiting
for pain to fade.
Time is no one's friend,
except for people with broken hearts.
The sun crests the horizon.
Visualize it washing
away the anchors I hold onto,
for the only reason
they're all I have left.
Empty handed I wait
beneath this blanket
bearing my warmth.
It lays cold with memories
spent together,
especially the night I conceived of a child
and she could not.

-collateral damage-

We met on Queen Anne
in the parking lot of Dick's
across from Seattle
Center. You wanted
the necklace
you gave to me
as collateral
for the drugs I fronted you.

I wish it was for something
more romantic, but my best
friend was right: he always
said I was too attractive
to be a drug dealer--
you can never tell
who your real friends are
and you can never tell
who really loves you.

It was raining
so I sat in my car
chain smoking Spirits
and putting the butts
into a coffee cup.
I got there early--
fifteen minutes--
and when that time
passed, I called
the phone of the guy
you were using.

No answer, but the voicemail
recording was pretty on point:
"I'm not here, but who really cares?
You're depressed, I'm depressed,

so what are we really doing here?
Leave me a message
and I might call back.
If I don't it's probably
because I'm depressed."

Even though I didn't
want to,
I left a message
Saying that you were late
and that if you're not there
by half past, I'm gone.
Half past came
and went.
I wasn't gone. I called
again, left no message.
But I sent a text
asking
where you were.
A bit later, I started the car,
finally ready to go.
A buzzing brushed my leg--
it was your text
saying you were on your way.
I replied with, "Okay."
And I waited
until you appeared from around
the corner. I could tell
it was you from fifty yards
at night. I got out of the car
and, I hoped,
casually
lit a another cigarette.

You walked closer
and I watched you
out of the corner of my
eye—never looking directly

at you. When I felt
like it was right,
I looked up. My smoke
wasn't even a third
finished.

How to best describe
the kaleidoscopic
tapestry of feelings
humming through
me when I saw your
face...

You said hi and I nodded.
I took my hand
from my pocket,
already holding the necklace.
I stretched out my hand
and you stretched yours.
The only physical
link
remaining
between us.

You asked me how I'd been
and I told you. Promotion
in my job that I started
right before I kicked you
out of my life. Working
on my poems, feeling better
than I had in months.

Then I asked about you.
Up to the same
shit is what I got
from what you said. Moving
from place to place
living for free. Job

"opportunities" were available--
I asked you what that meant--
you replied, "Stripping."

I asked about your mom
because, let's face it,
she might have been the best
thing about you. You said
her husband cheated
on her again. They were still
together. I wished I hadn't
asked. You went on to rail
against your step-dad
and your mom

and while you did it
I couldn't tear my gaze
from the light in your eyes.
Something in your pupils,
the blue in the iris,
the shape your lids
sculpted along the surface
of the sclera.
It was safe to say
I never wanted
the moment
to end.

I apologized for everything
that you saw as going
wrong. Then I said it was time
for me to leave.
I don't want to remember
if we hugged before
we parted. I feel like we did.
But let's say we didn't.

I told you to have a good

night. I really meant,
have a good life.

I hoped I'd never see you
again
and as I drove away
along Mercer street
the lights of the city
that I love
began to blur
I put the wipers
on mist.
But everything still bled
together.

-not today, satan-

You called me
from a number I didn't recognize.
Naturally in my curiosity
I answered the call.
I heard your voice through the phone,
immediately saw your face.
You asked me for something
and I said, "No."
Not today.
I'm still in love with you
but the difference now
is that I won't let it ruin my day,
my month,
or even my year.
Not today.
In the midst of loving you
I lost myself
and love
for myself.
Coffee and cigarettes,
the diet of hookers
and people who just
don't fucking care.
But not today.
I cut you out of my life
and I'm doing so much
better. 3 squares a day
and brushing my teeth
twice a day....even thinking
about exercising!
You wouldn't even recognize
me anymore.
I still think about how much easier
life would be if I were dead.
But not today.

My art is the way I live
and these words I write
to tell everyone how I feel.
I can't say it any other way.
I would like to be as honest
as the person writing these
things. But not today.
Some of the poems I write
aren't even about you!
And that might be the greatest
triumph
of all.
This one is about you,
but I'm not.
Not today.
Sometimes I still wish you were here
beside me, or driving my car...
helping me ruin my life
by giving it away to someone
other than me.
Sometimes I still wish to hear the words,
"I love you" from your lips.
But not today.

-true north-

More damaged than I ever thought
I was. Taking steps to heal
myself. Never knew it would take
this long or be this hard.
I've come to find lately that the hardest
decisions are the best ones to make
for myself. Easy decisions yield
no lasting satisfactions or authentic
rewards. Immediate gratification
has only eroded my work ethic,
sense of self, and health.
I can no longer cling to my insanity--
spinning my wheels, living the loop
of my actions has left me dizzy,
Lost in the woods with no moon
to see by. But the stars are still
out there in the blue black,
and all I need is the one that points
me North. This shining speck dwells
also in me. It is the knowledge
of what rings true in my soul.
I must steer following this
and give all of me to the pull
of what glints in the dark,
because that which has light
will always bring hope. And I can
do no wrong if I do what's best
for me.
-november 2017, seattle wa-

-golden hour-

Golden hour
descended on the valley
and splashed the stones
embedded
in the hills
and turned them
purple.

Golden hour
and the grass
of the pasture
where her family made
its living
glowed from the touch
of amber light.

Golden hour
happens
far before the day
they decided
to have me--
yet no day could be
as important.

Golden hour,
back in the hills
where blue stones
of agate are found,
the two first saw
each other.

Golden hour.
Is the term "destiny"
an appropriate term
for what happens

here, today?
Has it happened before?

Golden hour,
both atop horses,
I wonder sometimes
who saw the other
first.
I like to think the answer
is neither.

Golden hour,
same time, same place
reverberating
into eternity
for infinity.
A copy of a copy of a copy
but never diminished.

Golden hour,
the time where the sun
and moon
trade places
and are seen for a moment
together.

Golden hour
is here
and so are they--
I wonder if they knew
they'd fall in love
or if they already had.

Golden hour,
will either of them
be as young
as they are
now

again?

-to you-

One of my best friends told me a story
about being at a party
and seeing a really cute guy
and making the decision
not to talk to him.
As she was about to leave someone yelled
that they needed to get this guy to a bathroom.
It was the guy she'd seen.
He was totally off his head.
She said the story pertained perfectly
to me and how I'm attracted to so many people.
They all have qualities you're attracted to,
she said, but the doors aren't opened yet.

Is that true, my love? Is your head stuck
into a toilet right now,
purging you of bad decisions?
Am I my friend in this story, but making the other choice?
If I talk to you would it still be your head
or mine?
Or am I the guy totally off his head?

I've been doing better
but I've also been slipping.
I feel like I'm running out of gas,
getting tired.
I still do my yoga
and as you see I'm still writing poems.
I meditate every night
and welcome the dark stillness within.
Are you proud of me, my lovely?
I'm ashamed.
I'll have to think of a new name
to call you
because I've used all my others

on others.
I fear my karma will only come
when I think I've gotten everything I want.

I can't go on, I can't go on.
Okay, I'll go on.

To be the person I want to be.
That's what I want.
I still have rocks to uncover
inside
if I'm to unlock what I seek.

It's a strange thing to know
that later I will read this
to you someday.
The first step. Right there.
To know you are there.
And the keys?
They're buried beneath the rocks.

-end of an era-

the night before you left
we sat on the bench
at Kurt Cobain's house
and smoked lots of weed.
peri found a note his soul mate
who he's never met wrote
to kurt and left there in good faith
to be found by one of the greatest
souls i've ever met. "the sun has gone but
i have the light."

the next day you took off
to seek your fortune
in Portland
and do the thing that you love
with your little brother. and that
was the beginning
of the end
of an era.
the happiest times of my life.
"sunday morning is every day
for all i care."

before you left,
we smoked dmt,
fractals dancing
on the white walls
of my studio apartment,
sun poured
through the blinds
and gave me my first
real
idea of heaven.
you said you saw animals
parading across the ceiling,

getting to one side,
morphing into something else,
and then cantering back
to where it started.
"in a daze cuz i found god."

i still have a picture of us
in the car before the parting
of ways: you wearing a ten
gallon cowboy hat, tattoos
standing out stark
on your pasty white skin,
a look on your face,
something like surprise
mixed with wonder.
i'm wearing aviators
and my cap cocked back,
no worries in my world..
the past is a story
and it's my favorite one.
"the worst crime
is faking it."

i wish you hadn't left
and now you've changed--
so have i. it's the way
of the world
and it's the thing i hate the most.
everything changes
and that's my main gripe
with it all. i've failed
miserably on my new year's
resolution. "replace complaining
with gratitude." so much easier
said than done--and how am i
to give up the thing that i'm best at?
"i like to complain
and do nothing

to make things better."

i wished you all the best then
and i still do now. i just hate
that everyone moves away.
"i'm so happy
cause today i found my friends.
they're in my head."

-work in progress-

Sometimes we want someone
so badly, and after the dust settles
it turns out we didn't want
someone so much as we wanted
anyone. Winter is coming
and the days are shorter.
The rains are coming.
The long night.

I understand just as well
as anyone.
These are my dark months,
when the planet is farthest
away from its position
to the sun,
relative to the moment
I was born.
June babies don't do well
in winter.

Winter is coming
and our beds are cold.
They need warming
to weather the lengthy
night. What better than one
body? Two. I understand
the concept.
Your best friend tried
to set us up--
she did too good of a job.
It happened,
too soon,
too fast.

The first night we met,

I had you in my bed
and it was great.
You had me choke you
and you called me, "Daddy"--
all the things
I like.
But something wasn't right.

I went about ending it
wrong, I will admit. I wish
I'd been more mature
than I seem to be.
You messaged me
and I ghosted.
You're smart though
and you took the hint.
The next thing I saw of you,
you were back together
with your ex
and it all made sense.
You didn't want to be with
someone, you wanted to be
with anyone.

It's okay, beautiful creature,
we all want to be loved.
I hope you find solace
in the thing that used
to bring you pain. I'm sorry
if I added to that load.
I'm still learning, just
like
you.

-being a man child is easy-

Being a man child
is easy.
How did I get this far
not being able
to take care
of myself?
Skipping on the staples
of self care
and ignoring the things
that are good for me.
How did my parents
know what was good
for them
and what was good for me?
I stand in awe
of the people
who raised me.
To me they are wizards,
professionals
at life-ing.
They still step in to save
my ass
every once in a while.
I'm almost thirty
and only now
am I getting a handle
on things. Still under
a mountain of debt
and suffering from severe
procrastination.
But I'm getting better.
Baby steps, as the saying
goes. I have a savings,
pretty sizeable actually.
I have Healthcare,

thanks to the state
and the fact that I'm super
poor. Still in poverty.
My parents pay
for my phone
and my car insurance.
How will I survive
when they're gone?
This thought is terrifying
if I dwell on it
for too long.
Gratitude is not good
enough of a word
for what I feel for those
who brought me
into the world
and who continue to ease
my way.
I have to make list
after list
just to keep myself
on track.
I'm still just a kid
playing at being
an adult.
This is the truth
and I accept it.

-same-

This is what it is to be a millennial.
The vibes are heavy,
everyone stuck
in survival mode.
Real talk though.
We all want
to be in each other's lives
but we're not.
We don't see each other.
We work
all the time.
Entitled, my ass.
No such thing
as playdates anymore.
Or vacations,
for that matter.

An overheard quote
from my housemate,
"It's OG as fuck though dude,
I hate my life so fucking much."
Same.
Meme the pain away...
have you seen the meme
of the dog sitting
in a burning room?
The caption says,
"This is fine."

Hotter summers,
colder winters.
We are making twenty percent
less than our parents
in a world that costs
twice as much

to live in.

I live in a house
with eight other people.
We are all approaching
the age where we're off
our parents' insurance.
And we thought life
was tough
before.

Student loans
destroying our credit
and social media
allowing us to gloss
over the pain
we feel.

The fire-est of memes
are the ones that crystallize
our pain and suffering--
first world problems.
The struggle is real.
Are poets obsolete
now that we have memes?

I don't know whether
the world is causing
my anxiety
or if it's the progress
I'm making on my spiritual
path. I hope it's the former
because I'd hate
to be rewarded with a slap
in the face.
I want to throw up
half the time I go to eat.
Nervous fucking wreck.

The drugs I've done
have ended up
doing me. Nothing
that used to make me feel
good does anymore.
My mom has to be worried
about me. I know
she is
and I want to call her
and tell her
that I'm scared.
Maybe I don't
because I'm afraid
that she would say
she is too.

-reaching-

You asked me something last night.
It stirred my soul
and reminded me of my fortune:
"Loving me isn't so much fun, is it?"
I wish I would have had a better response
than the one I gave.

But, darling one, the fact of the matter
is this:
Love was never meant to be fun
and I pity the souls who sit
in their love and ignorance and have yet
to discover
the flip-side of the coin of love.
Those pure and untested lovers
will tremble and curse themselves
when the truth is revealed
about their fairy tale,
when they find that love
is so much like life.
How blessed I am to have found a love
that will take my life to perfect.

You sat there in your darkness and asked
a question bursting with light.
"Do you feel like the person you loved is gone?"
My love appeared
in front of my eyes, and I loved her even more
for having been so brave to ask a question
so terrifying. Because my love, the simple truth
is that no one can be brave without first being
scared.

You are there always, behind your
eyes. I smile at you even when they

are clouded over, because I know it brings out
your love. Even though it might annoy
your cloudy eyes, I see the movement
behind them, a stirring as if from beneath
water, something starved of breath
and swimming furiously toward
the promise of air,
and light.

-drugs-

The drugs aren't working
anymore. I mean, they still
get me high, but they don't
give me what I felt
from them before. Maybe
a good thing.
My poor brain,
I know I've done a number on it.
Even cigarettes zing
me now in a way they didn't before.

Am I going crazy?
Is that a real thing?
Can these drugs
make me nuts?
I mean let's face it:
crazy is in my family.
Dementia on both sides,
schizophrenia and a side
of chemical imbalance
to round it all off.
Oh, I almost forgot,
a couple of cases of bi
polar to make me feel
a little more than properly
fucked.

Native cultures believe
mental illness is a natural
aberration in a perfectly
healthy mind. They see it
as a reaction to environmental
input and an inability to reconcile
contradictions in the workings
of reality. Maybe I need to go

crazy, so I can find my way back?

The world feels more insane
every fucking day,
and so do I.
Nothing makes sense
and I'm feeling desperate
to get my bearings back.
I've already cut out meat
and marijuana. Now even dairy
and tobacco are fucking
with my body and my mind. Not
to mention, the drugs.
I feel like all the things I love
are slowly killing me.

They say you can get a lot higher
without drugs
than you can with drugs.
I didn't doubt it then,
but now I'm praying
it's true.
-august 2017, spokane wa-

-death trip-

I took three hits of blotter
after not tripping
for months. The paper was gold.
Wonka Golden Ticket
is what it said.

I didn't show the proper respect--
I'd forgotten what it was like to trip
and why we do it. I felt the come up.
Suddenly the person I loved texted me.
She wanted to come home--
I wasn't there, but I wanted her home
with me..
I told her as much--"Too bad you're high"
was what she replied.
And at that moment, I didn't want to be
high
anymore.

Now I'm not me--in my memory
I can't see what happened.
I'm flitting around, from past life
to parallel life--all these different selves...
fragments of my soul
and where they happened to land
in time. It looks to me like
I've always been a tragedy.
Flashback to the time I tripped
on twenty hits: sunshine, lots and
lots of sunshine. The happiest day
of my life. Feeling like I peaked
at twenty-six--two years past my prime
and a year before I'd committed
to twenty-seven more on my birthday.
What's it like to feel over the hill

at twenty eight?

Images of decay and death crowding my mind--
teeth slowly winnowing to slivers, corrupted
cells multiplying, and the idea of children
becoming more and more real. Clocks
are more threatening now and time
is no one's friend, except people
healing from broken hearts.

My friends afterward telling me
that I spun around
and around
until I broke the TV.
Thankfully it was 20 years old--
about time to be replaced.
And I was more than happy
to do it.
I remember someone stooping down
to talk to me--real or hallucination
I don't know:
"You're literally
trying to die, dude."
And I looked it in the eye and nodded,
saying, "I know."

-being good to myself is hard-

In the name of bettering
myself, I've made a list of goals.

First, start eating right.
Few people realize
how hard this is for me.
Not only does it cost
more than one would think,
But I don't get paid
as much as I need.
Every day I have to reassess
my food supply.
and make the decision
of whether or not I need to buy
more. Oh yeah, and the effort
it requires to make food.
Making food is so much better
when you can do it with someone
else. Not to mention the kitchen:
a mountain of dishes in each sink
and the trash is overflowing
because we have trouble
separating trash
and recycling.

Second, get a job.
Ever since i was young,
I've hated having a job.
Not because I don't like working
but because we have to pay to live...
the only species that does so.
Why do we think we're so different?
This and the fact that my taxes
fund wars where poor people
are bombed

and then turned away
when they come to our shores
for sanctuary. Thank god
this job is better than most.

Thirdly, brush and floss
twice a day. For many reasons,
self care has always been a struggle.
Maybe because it always
seemed like a chore,
rather than a way to tell myself
I love you...
I wish I'd had some real talk
about how much of an issue
my teeth would be.
I was always told,
"You'll regret it,"
to which I replied,
"Nuh uh."
...Uh huh.
Now I suddenly realize
I'm worth all the love
I can give to myself.
and besides, I'm always on
the lookout
for new ways to be mindful.

Lastly, get. Enough. Sleep.
Team No Sleep has been my crew
ever since I was young.
During summers I'd stay awake
with my little brother
for days on end
just to see how long
we could avoid sleep.
My first hallucinations,
and damn they were a trip.
I used to love staying up

late at night
when no one else was awake.
I still do.
I have to shove myself
into bed every night
before I'm ready.

The hardest things in life
seem to be the ones
that will pay the greatest
rewards. But not without
effort. I battle with myself
and argue back and forth
in my own head
about whether or not
I should smoke
this next cigarette,
or if this coffee I'm craving
can be done without.
This phase is still
an infant..
I wish I could say
I love it,
but so far it mostly feels like chores.

-my addictions-

I know I should stop smoking
these cigarettes. I'm going
on three years now, but I'm so close
to having a voice like Tom Waits.
Rawr.
Can't stop now.

Plus I love the ritual
of slapping a new pack,
tearing the cellophane
like I did when buying
a CD when I was younger.
Flip the top and tear out
the gold foil. Flip the second
and third in the front row
upside down.
One for good luck,
the other, a good fuck.

Plus I feel like
I'm worse at sex now.
If that's not a good reason to quit,
what is?
Maybe it's not the cigs. Maybe
it's because I jerk off too much.
Porn makes it easy to cum.
A couple of different friends told me
watch less porn and stop jerking off.

Instant gratification is ruining sex.
People having orgasms
in front of a screen--
Oxytocin, Cupid's arrow,
making me fall in love
with a glowing screen

instead of a beating heart.

I just had sex
when I told myself
I wasn't going to this season.
I smoked a Camel after.
It was good.
The cigarette anyway.
The sex was good, too
for me.
I'm not sure how it was for her.
But that in itself
isn't a good sign.
At least I didn't watch porn
and use it to get off,
right?

I was much better at this a few years ago.
I only smoked
when others offered.
And I could fuck for hours.
Now I'm out of breath
and out of desire.
Is this getting old?
I promised my friends until 54.
Something's gotta give.
I want more passion.
Less poison.

-requiem-

I went through my friends list today
deleting people. Such a cruel phrase.
Here's something worse:
a lot of people on that list
are dead. I already wish I hadn't,
but I deleted some of them
because they're already deleted. But look:
here they are in this poem.

I met one of them at the Gorge.
I gave him his first dose of acid
for free. He fought hard to pay for it.
I took his money. I gave him the hit,
then I ate the dollar bill in front of him.
He chased me around,
laughing,
yelling, Why did you do that?
Because.

Another on the list, I didn't know very well.
Many of my friends knew him well
The smile in the profile picture speaks
volumes to the quality of his soul.
We flowed a couple times together
and that was it.
Next I heard he died from pills.
Can we not do this anymore?
Please?

The third is the closest to my heart.
He was the one who got me into selling.
The best job I ever had.
He grew the best weed and gave me the courage
to leave someone who was staining my soul
the color of rust.

He had more wisdom in one of his cuticles
than I had in my whole being.
He too lost to drugs. But here he is now.
Farewell
and hello,
Superstar.

I've seen my death many times before,
but it's never happened. Not yet.
I wonder what the reactions will be
when that day comes. Probably as varied
as there are people.
I abandoned a cigarette to write this poem.
Please let it be said of me
when I'm gone
that my addictions were less important to me
than my art.

-feburary 2018, seattle wa-

-not tonight-

It feels like I haven't written
in a week.
I just wrote
the other night.
A friend hits
me up and asks
to hang out.
I haven't done anything
all day--
except morning yoga
and read a book. And ate
some food I bought
at the grocery store
and cooked at home
like a real adult.
I still feel tired
so I tell him I can't.
Well, I tell him
that I'm good.
Some other time, I say
and feel bad. Guilt

is feeling bad
for doing what we want
when someone else
wants something else.

This passes.
I recline against
my pillows, under orange
lights on my ceiling,
listening to the sound
of nothing.
My breath.

-I don't want a glamorous life-

as my idea of myself
as something irreplaceable
and all important
shrinks,
the possibilities for what it I might become
expand.
That becomes less important
as I accept what my life is.

For people to know who I am
used to be a clenching, burning
wish, but now it seems a fate
worse than death.
I am not as important
as the thing you hold
in your hands,
the words you are reading.

All these nice things that people
have are surely nice to have
for them. Even nicer for me
to know they have them
and to know that the things
I want are not things--
and are already on their way
to me.

This bliss comes in waves
but the lows are never
as low as they were
when I didn't love myself.

-equilibrium-

I've been having a problem
with my brain. Close
to always a phantom
of a thought, there in moments
of an unoccupied mind.
A feeling of not being quite
on center. Like the earth
is slightly off its axis
or the fear that one day
it will be.
Irrational flutter of panic
tickling around the same
part of my brain
that the anxiety comes from,
sharing space, a vision
of a cartwheeling world
full of vertigo.
Like one day out of the middle
of nowhere, I'll be so dizzy
I will have to hold
onto the face of the Earth
to keep from falling off.
What is this strange pathology?
My high school band teacher
once had wind blowing
into one of his ears
for so long that when he stood up
he couldn't hold his balance
and fell straight over.
Is it something in my ears
or just something in my head?
I haven't lost balance yet
but every step I take
has me on alert.
I ask myself

I ask my brain
what is wrong with it.
Is this another part
of the process
or am I alone on this one?
Maybe it's a reflection
of the fact that I feel
off balance. Too far
this way or that—I'm standing
on one end of the teeter
totter and trying to level
things out by running
to the other side
and back again.
Please tell me this will
end before it all does--
it's hard to keep going
to sleep at night,
telling myself,
"The sky isn't falling,
you're just growing."

-from the 'about me' part of my okcupid profile-

hello, I am called ry.
I am a human
in a semi constant
existential crisis
about climate change
and Earth's diminishing ability
to sustain human life. I write
poems about this and other topics.
I love laughing and dancing
more than anything. I am often found
among trees. I'm 5'6"
but you'd swear I was 5'8".

-fire medicine-

My best ideas always come
when I stare
into the guts
of a burning fire.
It leaps
and licks the air
with orange and red
tongue.
I watch.
It gives voice
to thoughts that come
only now. Smoldering coals
fading from hot orange
to black
and back.
I hear the breath
sounds of the ocean
behind and feel
the rise
and fall
in my chest.
It's then
I realize
the fire is breathing
too.

-alley scene-

An asphalt alley runs
behind where I work.

I sit outside and smoke
my cigarette regardless
of the weather.

Lately it's been pouring
rain and I gather my legs
to my chest and puff.

During summer, sunlight
bounces from alley walls
and illuminates my smoke.

Whatever happens out
there happens here,
but with a bubble of shelter.

I look out from my alcove,
nearly clear
of the reach of the rain.

I try not to think
in words or boxes--
they don't seem to belong.

Each scene is the same
in how it's different.
The cycle shows its face.

So glad to be here,
a witness--
not a judge.

-dragging myself over coals-

Just dragging myself over coals
because reasons.
How do those guys in India
walk on them
so casually?
Hothothot, hothothot
the heat of my shame,
one of my favorite phrases
of mine
if I have to pick.

I sit from afar and watch these women
who I could be in love with
if I gave myself the chance.
And if they gave me one.
Instead I spend series of one
nights because I've come to learn
the future is a lie.
Still lying awake at nights
in my comfy bed
with the heater on,
dragging myself over coals,
in between dreams
of the open road,
no rent to pay, no job to go to
and no one telling me what to do.

And poems, poems poems
for days.

I love you because you're just like me
but also just like you.
I love you because you are there
to be loved.
I know you want it too.

I love you because you'd hold
a coal in your palm
if it meant that no one else had to.
We are failures
of this self love thing we claim.
That's why everyone
loves us.
I love you because I'd want to hold the coal
for you
and you'd want to hold it
for me.

Maybe we could share it
just like this:
hold out your hand,
I'll hold out mine.

-thanksgiving poem, 2017-

I want to write a really important
poem about America and being
part Indian but much more white
than Indian. But I'm afraid it won't
be good enough or sound important
enough or that it will come off sounding
like I'm appropriating
a culture.

It's almost Thanksgiving. Last year
on that day Natives were tortured
with dogs, sprayed with water in sub
zero temperatures. Today
the pipeline they sought
to stop spilled hundreds
of thousands
of gallons
of oil.

Is it too late
or improper
to say,
"We told you so"?

Vindication never feels as good
as you think it will.
Hindsight makes perfect
vision
most of the time.

I marched in Seattle
against the Black Snake
and heard testimony
from brothers and sisters
who stood at Standing Rock

and were asking for our help.
I posted on Facebook
and watched live streams
of the conditions
and brutality
that went on there.
I shared articles
and sent letters
and signed petitions
and did my best
to make political
decisions with my money.
I did my best.
It wasn't enough.

My blood boils
as I remember
words written
by a poet from the Sixties.
Something about what
have they done to the Earth?
What have they done to our
poor sister? Ravaged
and plundered
and raped her
and bit her.

I feel the hurt of the land.
My heart is its heart,
has come from its heart.
This land is not my land
this land is not your land--
we were never meant to own
something this eternal.
Meant as stewards
for what we have poisoned,
we will all come to know
its pain.

Some of my ancestors
were residents, keepers,
cherishers of this place.
I remember being asked
what tribe my ancestors
were from. Since she seemed
to care, I said that they
were part of the Blackfoot
Nation. She laughed and said,
"That's what everyone says."

In times like these
a curious rustling
occurs from within
the basin of my soul.
Minority bits of my blood
rage and war against the part
that isn't from these shores.
Red vs red, all blood
is blood. My heritage
a microcosm of the planetary
tableau. On my surface
white is what you see--
the same exists for our world
today. Native narratives
buried beneath the white
lies about the land of milk
and honey.

-seven generations-

The natives believed
in thinking about the next
seven generations
when thinking about the world
they were making.
That is the person I want
to be: considering
the livelihood
of people I'm never going
to meet. The ultimate
form of empathy.
They are my relations
and this Earth will remain
for them. Will they be
nourished the same as I
have been? Thoughts
like these keep me up
some nights
and it's not til the sun
comes up do I sleep.
Sunrise, a symbol
of hope
for those who would see
the dawn of a new age.
Never forget
we are all family,
coming from the Earth,
and returning there
in the end.

-reality rules-

My reality is breaking
down. Nothing
feels as real
as it did
compared to when I was
young.
We're always so sure
of what is
and isn't.

Rules and their exceptions
we absorb
until we're full
and certain.

The real work comes
in the form of love
and what poses as it.

Now that I know the names
of things
I learn new facts--
there's more reality
in what lies behind
my eyes
when they close.

Sit silent
in the dark
and hear the echo
of what resounds
in space.
Strengthen the tether
between the darkness
and the sound that made

the universe.
A piece of it is within
and sits patient.
It doesn't demand to be
recognized--
it whispers beneath the din
of the waking world.
Some find their way
here on their own.
Others are shown the way.
Silence,
the language of the real,
speaks without
lips or tongue.

Reality is somewhere
beyond the reach
of false streetlight haloes
and machine sighs
of passing cars.

-i'm not crazy-

Spiritual awakenings
aren't all they're cracked up
to be. I saw a meme
the other day...
It had two panels.

The title of it was "What you think
a spiritual awakening is like
vs.
what a spiritual awakening is really
like."

The first panel shows a woman
sepia-toned
in full lotus,
her eyes closed,
soft focused,
so serene,
hands pinched
in the classic mudra.
So peaceful.
This is how we see Buddha
in our minds,
such a peaceful state
he's in as he realizes
that all of this
is illusion.

The closest I come to peace
is when my eyes
are closed.
I'm not meditating.
Instead it's when I sleep,
even better when I don't remember
my dreams. The sweet dark

bliss of lost time.
Please don't wake me up...
five more minutes
and then I'll
be good.
Don't make me
do stuff.

The second panel shows a woman
curled up in a ball,
tears streaming down,
and the subtitle says,
"I'm not crazy,
I'm not crazy."
I wonder
did the Buddha
think he was going crazy?
Revealing the world to be nothing
but maya,
illusion,
finding that it was only
him
alone
in a funhouse
full of mirrors?
Reflections of himself
talking to themselves,
the same story
from different points
of view?

That feels more right--
the deeper the rabbit
hole goes,
the more crazy I find myself
becoming. Anxiety a constant
threat, any time I'm relaxing
it's whispering to me

that I'm not doing enough.
I used to be content
with the way things were
or at least the way I was.
But even that's not true--
seekers are always seeking
and always will seek,
regardless of how things seem
fine. Things aren't fine
and neither am I.
Gotta do more,
gotta be more,
gotta do better.
Show them
show her
that I'm fine
being alone.

Let go of everything
and watch it come back.
The law of attraction
states this. Don't want
and it will want you.
What a fucking rigged
game this is. Apathy
is the secret to life.
I don't care
so you will.
Does this make sense
to anyone else?
Love with ambivalence,
not interested in the result.
Have I got this right?
Loneliness will set you free
but what good is freedom
when you're alone?

1. WHAT DO YOU PERCEIVE TO BE THE MEANING OF LIFE?

2. WHAT IS YOUR IDENTITY?
3. WHAT IS YOUR PURPOSE?

-a meditation-

I meditate on
an image of you blowing
me a kiss--
your almond eyes
in shape and color
creasing a little
at the edges,
the beginnings
of the making
of the expression
I love--

A kiss,
lightly,
against
the part
of your hand
that has seen
less sun.

Next,
and this
is the part
I love--
you tilt your hand
forward
and here is the part,

You close your eyes
slowly,
lightly,
as if to form
the beginning
of a first
kiss.

Like you feel
it like I do.

Eyes closed,
your lips
make the perfect
shape,
the one that goes on
forever
and air sings
through your lips
and carries your kiss
and this
brings
me
peace.

I'm sorry I kissed you--
or rather
I'm sorry
I didn't ask.
I broke my own rule.
Now I'm paying
for it.
I always ask
before I kiss.
It might sound
lame, but I believe
in respect.

The mushrooms
and booze
definitely had an effect--
but what it really was:
the way your eyes
narrow and lines show
in your face
that weren't there

before I made you laugh.

When you touch me
on my arm, leaving
tingles.

The way the light
in your room
caressed your face
the way I
wanted to.

I think I overstepped
but on nights
like this
I think
about how even after
we kissed,
you still blew
me kisses.

That
gives
me
Peace.

-moon experience-

The moon is still full
tonight.
I saw her
driving in the car
with a friend.
She mentioned its beauty
in the same moment
I was thinking it.

Emotions are charged by the moon.
So many souls
I hold deeply
in my heart. They all proclaim
their love for her
in different moments
in different ways.
Some have tattoos
of her phases.
Some wear clothing
bearing her face.
Others write poems
about her beauty.

I saw her again driving back
from dropping my friend
off at her house.
Maybe it's because of the super moon
but as I coasted down the hill
toward my house,
it looked so close--
like I could touch it,
pluck it from the sky--
an opalescent orange
hanging from backlit
boughs whose leaves

were breaths of clouds.

I laid in bed wishing I could sleep
and watched the clouds
wisp by. Moonlit, they glided
across the sky
like ferries floating across the Sound.
After a time, the cloud assumed
a shape—from where I lay
I saw a vision of a man,
just the head
at first,
then,
I saw a shoulder, then an arm
reaching out
in my direction.
His chest emerged
and he floated
like this
across the sky, arms wide open,
head tilted upward.
The only thought that crossed my mind:
"Open yourself up."

-silver cord-

I had a hard time falling
asleep last night.

And when I did, you were
in my dream.
The room was dark--
I laid a hand
on your foot
pretending to tickle,
but you didn't flinch.
I left my hand there

on your foot.

I felt
your foot
within
my hand.

I

felt

it.

We sat there
like that.

My heart

my heart

beating

in my chest.

Then you moved
and the world

shifted.

Your hands pressed
against my chest
and I felt
sweet breath
on my lips.
We kissed and the world
turned upside down

right side

up.

I'm afraid to tell
you who you are
so
maybe we'll just
keep this

our secret.

You probably know
already.

That's what you do.
You drink coffee
and know things.

We've always been good
at speaking
without words.

I woke up--

I hadn't slept
for more than an hour.

I wondered:
"Do we even dream
during that dot of sleep?"

Then I remembered
some words exchanged

a lifetime ago.

You told me once
that you

can dream

and find the astral bodies
of those you love.

I bet
you can read my mind
from clear over here.
I don't need
to ask
the question

that kept me up

the rest of the night.

-mushies are our thing-

The first time we ate
mushrooms—we were living
in that studio in Bellevue
across the street
from Nintendo campus.
I didn't know what to expect.
They hit.
I knew I needed to be
outside. We hopped halfway
across the street
to the median covered
in grass and trees--
a safe zone, a green
oasis amidst a concrete
desert.

Connection re-forged, we sat
cross legged and waves
of wild wonder washed
over our limbs and in the half
light from streetlights,
waterfalls miraged our vision.
Coronas popped in our eyes,
halos blessed upon us
from the night's lights—natural
and not.

I started trying to talk
my way into making
wonder reality.
You broke in
saying the perfect thing.
"I know you want to talk
right now but I just want
to run."

I looked at you
and took off running
down the street.

When I was younger
I ran every single day.
Running never felt
so right than with my twin
flame by my side. We whooped,
banshees screaming through
Microsoft campus. Miles
were nothing because all
there was
was
Now.

We stopped in a copse
of trees and doubled over
panting together as one--
I ended up telling you
how much I love you.
I don't remember it all.
One phrase still rings
through time
crystallized in memory:
"I would commit genocide
for you."
Today it's just as true.
You started crying. I wish
that I could help you hold
onto the coursing glory
of that night when we basked
in the glow of each
other's beauty
and light.

Independence Day
a couple years later

we sat on top
of that hill
above her parents' place
and watched fireworks
from miles away
and we remembered
mushrooms after midnight
and I said it was my favorite
trip we'd taken. You agreed,
saying that mushies are
our thing.

-december 2017, seattle wa-

The Sun

-the science of love-

we define ourselves
by our pain. putting locks on thoughts
of what is possible. i've been sad
for so long that i'm finding
it difficult to let go. not of anyone
or any thing, but to leave
my hold on a feeling that kept me safe
and secure in the knowledge
that there was nothing i could do
to make things better.

it's romantic, isn't it, to bask
in the murky, quiet glow
of a cave where no light
offends our eyes, to sit
like a monk, fasting
from light and basking
in one's own suffering?
i fed myself a paralytic
and it worked like a charm--
almost like heaven for someone
who is terrified of change
and effort.

bravery is just another word
for stupidity, is what i would
tell myself when the thought
of going outside would come
to me. so i sat in my cave
and fasted until, slowly,
almost imperceptibly,
my hunger for what lies
beyond grew into its own desire.
with no food and no light,
my soul had begun to feast

on itself.

was it courage or self preservation
that drove me toward that moment
that finally changed it all,
when i ventured to the mouth
of my cave, at first, and then
gradually into the light to seek
something that would sustain
this body, this life, this soul
better than my cave. motion
is greater than paralysis

and a body that is at rest tends
to stay at rest, while the body
that moves is fed by its own
drive. the first step is the most
important and if you aren't careful
you will be swept away by momentum,
kinetic energy and inertia--gravity
becomes your ally and you are now
afoot and lighthearted upon the open
road, the science of spirit

at work, inspiration and intuition
dovetailing together to create
the only real kind of magic.
built into the fabric of nature,
i am become a vessel of this magic
that has many names--nature, magic,
spirit, love--but is known by all.
magic is far from automatic
but its roots reside in development
of habit. the more i love, the more i am.

-maybe that's why they call it fall-

I used to think that summer was my favorite.
It might be fall. I sit in my bed
that overlooks my street.
My windows are open,
a better way to fight against disease.
The birds' voices are still coming
to me, though the heat has passed.
Wispy clouds lighten the sky
as the sun passes through
and falls on tops of the trees,
some whose leaves are green
and others yellow and orange
and some lay fallen
on the ground.

Season of valuable lessons.
Seek to be like the trees—
look there and witness
how to avoid lamenting
loss of what used to be
part of your being. You must let go
in order to begin again. The things
that have outgrown their use
must be shed in order for the new
to come. More is learned from loss.

How are we to know abundance
by having everything we've wanted?
Wanting isn't needing—
abundance isn't surplus.
It's the state of having everything
you need. This season where leaves
make a multicolored carpet,
a tapestry of let go things. Let it all
go. See what comes back.

Like the leaves, you might find
what you let go coming back.

-happy thought-

Today was the first day
of fall. I drove
through a huge puddle
in the spot on the hill
where I know a puddle
will be every day it rains.
It's my routine—anyone
who has been in my car
knows the drill.
If there's a puddle big
enough to be called
a puddle in that spot,
I'll drive through it,
delighting like a child
in the splash it makes,
the perfect curving,
slicing arc it makes
through the air. Whoever
is in the seat next
to me usually laughs
too. Almost without
fail. What is it about making
splashes that delights
us so much? Aging,
we forget the simple
pleasures of our youth,
practicalities taking precedence
over play. These past couple
years I've forgotten
what it means to play.
Peter Pan with amnesia,
every year at October,
my roll would slow
and I would hesitate
to even dip my toe

into the now cold
waters of life
and the changing
of seasons. Even the leaves
could not delight me—I knew
what lay in store—months
of cold and rain.
Somehow I've remembered
my happy thought—and every
puddle now a challenge. I leap
forward, cold water
and wet socks be damned.
It feels like I'm become
someone else
again, and why
shouldn't it—all
I've done is come back
to myself.

-saturn return-

I've never looked at *The Great*
Gatsby the same way since someone
told me it was the story
of a man at the end
of his twenties. Despite that I still
haven't gone back and re-read
with that in mind.
Maybe I'm scared
of what I'll realize.

I'm almost halfway through
my twenty-ninth year
and the clock looks like
it's ticking faster.
I looked it up online
and Saturn makes its return
halfway through December
of this coming year.

I have less than a month
to prepare myself
for what is on its way--
if you believe in such things.
In a sea of churning change
where nothing looks the same,
the chaos said to be a symptom
of Father Planet's return
is the only alignment that shines

its light and gives me direction
in which to flow. At one time
I was tweaked about turning twenty--
but I still behaved like a kid--
a full decade of fucking off
and fucking up. Credit through

the floor and debt crashing
through the roof. I'm sitting
here in the mess I made

and the reality of thirty staring
me in the face. Ultimatums
zapping my brain into action
that I'd never considered.
"Time to grow up"
is what I'm hearing from somewhere
inside my head. "But..I'm Peter
Pan," I say to the voice,
which responds in a tone
that sounds like a shrug:
"It's up to you, but
it's not true what they say: The good
don't die young, but the dumb ones do."

But change has already started--
two years ago I was on everything
but skates. This day last year
I asked for a fortunate accident
with a city bus. This year--
look at me.
I haven't sold drugs in months,
I have a job with taxes and I brush
my teeth at night.

So here I am tonight
in my room wondering
if the storm was early
or if I'm just in its eye. The reason
humans came so far isn't that they
were smart. They adapted to change
and changed to adapt. Like the shark
death comes with the stopping of swimming.

But now while I wait

for the actual day
of the return of the father
planet who ate his children
in myths of the ancients
I float as lonely as a cloud
over the mountains that were
mole-hills in my mindscape
until attention swelled their size.

Needing to be addressed:
what gauntlets will be thrown
down to test my mettle?
Will I lose my job
again or will there be another
teenage girl with a four letter
word for a name waiting
to feed me another lie about love?

Will the pressure of living
off so little push me back
to the job I had selling smiles?
Or will living a life
with sex in the cross
hairs deliver me something
worthy of being called life
shattering? Maybe I'm asking
the wrong questions as I wait

for Saturn's return. Maybe I should
ask why I hold so tight
to this idea of youth
and how I was taught
to value it above the experience
of age. Every day I learn
and the words of the sages
sink and stick to my brain
as they never had before.

I must shift my focus
from the preservation of my
image to the anticipation of knowledge.
No one was ever saved
by the lack of blemishes
on his face—the world
has never truly needed Adonis
or James Dean. Babylon prays
at the altar of false idols

and I do not intend to be
one of those. Let me be
instead an elder who sits
cross legged on the floor
in the shadows who speaks
soft from somewhere in his chest,
a place of love, to remind
those of smooth skin that worship
of beauty must be with closed eyes.

It now becomes evident,
the only thing I fear
is the destruction of my self--
not in death, but in dismantling
what my ego pushed me to be.
Death is coming and the idols are dead.
I can only point my aim
in the direction of my higher self--
releasing who I am to become who I still may be.

-winds of change-

Trees are such an inspiration.
They bend and bend
and bend, but rarely ever
break. Roll with the punches,
go with the flow—if the roots
are strong, the wind will not win.

The air was still earlier,
with lots of rain. I drove
my housemate to work
so he could avoid the wet.
I like doing nice things
when I can spare my time.

Nature moves like we move.
We don't witness grass growing
before our eyes—but it's growing
every single second, unending
reaching of life. And so it is
with us.

We don't recognize the change
in others or sometimes ourselves
day by day, unless something
catastrophic comes, forcing
our hand. Disease, death,
injury--all tempests blowing about.

Prepare for the storms surely coming--
strengthen yourself and strengthen
your roots. Drink water, bend
with breezes that merely train
you for hurricanes. Your inner peace
is never assured.

-a zen poem about baseball-

I love baseball.
The ultimate zen master
sport. Perhaps the reason
people have grown
ambivalent toward
it's immense subtlety:
look down at your smartphone
for a moment, and suddenly:
a home run,
a double play,
a strikeout,
you've missed the golden
moment...a piece
of the highlight reel.

Okay, now watch: the pitcher
sets, the batter waits,
everything is still, a placid
pond's surface, waiting
for a ripple to spawn.
Here comes the pitch...
and now the infinitude
of possibility--will it be hit,
will it reach the catcher,
will it be fouled off
out of bounds beyond
the reach of all? There are infinities
within the finities of the game.
All or nothing, alpha and omega
exist here, hanging in the balance
between foul and fair and ball
and strike. One must prepare
for everything
and nothing.

Zen master sport for sure:
one must always be aware,
mindfulness at full display.
One on first, one on third,
one out, where am I going
with the ball if it's hit
toward me? Calculations
and all numbers of tuning
in amidst the stillness
on the top of the pond
that is the diamond.
You lose focus in this game
for one second,
and you commit an error.

Maybe it's different
for those who have never
played. I can't speak for them--
all I can speak for is experiencing
the smell of a leather glove
as you encapsulate your face
with it, smelling the hide
and oil, becoming one
with this new appendage
that will be your best friend
through these diamond times.

And how to speak of perfection
in this game of Zen
when you're from Seattle
but to offer the name
"Griffey" in hushed
and reverent tones?
The Kid, the symbol of unwashed
joy, the owner of the nineties,
10 golden gloves in a row
and a swing whose arc
was so pristine

it was basically Fibonacci
in action.

If this doesn't convince
of the beauty inherent:
I can only offer one more
image. Last year of little
league...all star game...
we are down by one...
bottom of the sixth...one man
on. I'm in the dugout,
hat inside out and perched
on my head--rally cap
style--superstition powering
our intention. My friend Travis
is at the plate. Every single eye
on the ball. The pitch comes,
a PING! of rawhide on aluminum
and the white of the ball
tearing across the sky
and over the fence.
Hearts shoot to throats
and adrenaline tears
through all. We rush
the plate and greet our hero,
tackling him to the ground
amidst a storm of cries,
and shouts and laughter.

-muse-

You.
An inspiration,
a spark
for a lightbulb,
a current
with which to run
toward a future
full of fairy tales
where the heroine
saves herself.

A source
the depths of which
can only be fully
fathomed in dreams
and then mostly
forgotten, only the breath
of which remains
on the surface
like a scar, a healed
reminder of the power
of art mirroring
my life.

Knotted hair, a symbol
of the magic kept secure
within our minds—
a rejection of the vanity
of a crumbling paradigm.
New beauty for a new
world. A new view
for blossoming times.
Fairy locks adorn
the crown divine.

These lines an ode
to the muses
of the muse.
Seeds are planted
and with care sown--
the harvest will come
and beauty be known.

-samhain-

The clock struck Samhain
and I ate some mushrooms--
a little more than a microdose--
and then I went to sleep.
I had to work in the morning.
I spent three hours dreaming
of darkness, amorphous shapes
and a woman with pale skin
in a bathroom that was all
white. She had black hair
and was naked, and on
her knees, facing the tub,
which was filled with black
liquid. I had no idea
what she wanted. She dunked
herself in the black liquid,
submerging herself
to the shoulders. When she came
back up, the liquid ran all the way
down her back, and she looked
back at me, saying with her eyes
what she wanted me to do.
So I did it. I woke up in the dark
still aroused. Mushrooms do that
to me. Awake in the dark, bodies
contorting, different positions
presented to me on the tapestry
above my bed.

I love women who are obsessed
with death. Witchy women,
one might call them. Tonight
the Goddess descends into women.
Samhain—The Witch's New Year.
A New Year because as things begin
their death, the promise of new life

is born. Fertility is born of decay.
The wisest of witches—the ones
I love—know this too, that the dead
never truly leave. I strive to retain
the thought—amidst all dying
therein begins
the renewal of all things.
As a fire engulfs a forest
and is extinguished, so the pinecone
releases its seeds to begin again.

Liminality describes
the line between the worlds.
Spirits, faeries,
echoes of the pagan gods
and nature spirits make their return
and must be appeased for us
to survive. Souls of our our dead
return tonight seeking reminders
of a warm home and laughter of friends.
We used to prepare a space for them
at the head of our table and eat
our meal in silence, reverence
for the dead. When was the last
time I sought silence to remember
my dead? My grandfather died
years ago, and I feel each year
he comes back to me, bit
by bit. I use phrases of his,
my worldview merges with his.
I believe he will come back
to me tonight.
What will I learn?

Time stops here, tonight. Past,
present,
future,
all are one.

In the past, on this day,
we remember our dead.
May we do so again
to remember the value
of our grief
and the worth
of our lives.
Who gave us this life?
Our thanks go to they
who came before
and tried to teach us
what experience had taught
them. Celebrate renewal,
dance into the spiral
of time, close your eyes--
glimpse a vision
of what we will create.

-premonitions-

A friend of mine given
to premonitions told me
I'm meant to have children.
Or maybe just one,
but all the same--
a child. According to her
it's meant to happen.

Pronouncements like these
cause a certain wondering
of what is true.

It's true I am a being of love.
A man who has wisdom to give--
guidance and examples to live by.

It's true I have found what life
is about. Simplicity, in all its forms.
Truth, love, loyalty, not worrying
too much about what other people think.

It's true I would have raised
her child if it had been mine--
dropped everything and moved
to Texas if that was her wish.
My life wouldn't have been mine
and that would have been life.

It's true images of a child
miraged my mind—blue,
blue eyes and curls, curls of angel-
colored hair. A smile that melted gold
and hearts. A name weirder
than my own, if that were possible.

It's true I looked at baby clothes
the day before she had the abortion
I paid for. Thirty three
percent chance that it was mine
but I mourned like I'd killed my own
myself. Try to remember

it's true souls never die-
they are recycled in reservoir
of reincarnation. That soul remains
above my head,
aethered and waiting
for its moment to arrive,
an avatar half of me, half of her,

wherever she is.

I hope it's a girl.

-may 5 2018, seattle wa-

-for anyone who has felt personally victimized by feminism-

I mean, seriously, what's the big
deal, anyway? I mean, they're allowed
to drive cars and go to college
and vote in elections, aren't they?
They even get charged less
for car insurance!
What do they have to bitch
about? I don't see the big deal.

Today I was online
and saw a post made by a friend
of a friend. The post was another
report of a random dick pic
sent to her inbox. The internet's
equivalent of dropping trou'
in front of a complete stranger
and declaring, "Look at this!
You know you want it."
Unsolicited penis pictures-- a perfect
portrait of the privilege
of having a penis. Who in their right
mind would turn that down?
I told my friend to put him on blast--
but then thought better
and told her to friend the guy's mother
and send her a screenshot of her son's penis.

I've never had a sister, at least
not by blood. And I've fucked up
a few times as well.
But at the same time I've never
forgotten that my sisters are people
too. We learn early on that violence
is a term of endearment and desire
just a compliment. Why feel bad

when we're just showing
how we feel? You should be happy
I'm showing you attention at all.

We've learned how to make violence
out of words. A conversation
that goes from "Hey beautiful
 to "ugly bitch I hope you get AIDS
and die" when no response is given.
I wish I was exaggerating, but we
all bear witness to everyday
vitriol like this. What demons we breed
by turning souls into objects.

If I had a daughter I would
present her with her very own can
of mace, and a set of brass
knuckles as soon as she was old
enough to use them. And I would
go into a lonely room and weep
at the necessity of it at all.
I will do my best to create
a change, but one must prepare
to confront the way things are.

My mother always told me she prayed
for two sons. She got what she wanted,
and when asked about her wish, she said
it was because boys were easier
to deal with. I accepted that answer
until now--I wonder if she gave
me the truth, or if there lies
a darker truth beneath her response.
Is there something she's never shared,
a fear she never wanted her own children
to have to face?

So long ago we abandoned the Goddess

in the name of a single God--
jealous and vengeful, and told ourselves
we were made in his image.
How to recover from amputating
one of our limbs? Do you feel off
balance? I still have phantom
pain in my lost limb, so is it truly
gone? One is the loneliest
number, and it has always taken
two in order to create a life.
We all came from a mother, with help
from a father. Never forget
that you were forged and formed
in the body of the Goddess.

-it takes time to become a god-

You know it's time to read
some poetry
and it's gonna feel good too
after it feels terrible.
Watching these gods
of the word
do their thing.

And it comes
in an entropy of ease
and weightlessness
you know
as of now
that you could only achieve
in your dreams.
But you never see the slashing
and cutting they did--
the hours and years,
grains in the hourglass
that filtered downward
as their mountains
in your hands
grew higher
until they became
the Olympus you witness,
the book in your hands,
the lines that slay
and eviscerate
your sense of yourself
as a poet. You are a fake

you are convinced
as the book shakes
in your palsied hand.
Take care

and have faith,
young one,
surely your grains are falling
and building your own Olympus
or Rainier--
the second one has lava
and can erupt
any minute.

They stand in awe every time
you are out
and the mist clears
to reveal your peak.
Schoolchildren do drills
in the event of your eruption.
Memory fades
but awakens
when the match is struck.
Take care and have faith.
It takes time to become a god.

-the subjective reigns supreme-

Here we go here we go here we go
another cigarette abandoned
to write this fucker

I can do it I can do it I can do it
and so can you
positive affirmations is all I do
today
because I you we
have to take back our brains
from the black hole
that manifests
in bright white LCD
a juxtaposition of the highest degree
we are drawn to the light
like bugs that crackle sizzle pop
on the electric fence
of the bright blue forever of never

can you dig the gold that is buried
here in these lines
can you be hip to this lingo daddy-o
or is it easier to resort to one word responses
same
rekt
true
it's all the same but
right now I feel like my hair is on fire
and we're walking on a wire
so thin that from there
in your seat you might say where?

The subjective reigns supreme
and you can't tell me otherwise
look what all your facts have brought

you me we us to
complacency is our bread and I can't believe
it's not butter.
Mad (un)willingness cartwheels from someone
who has never taken gymnastics
are here to stay

finally feeling inspired again
and fuck it feels good to have a tongue
loose and ready for something other
than eating pussy
though that's fun too
and maybe afterward we can all stop being
so fucking uptight about words like pussy
and penis and see that we're all the same
and it's only a sin if you hurt someone else.

Get out of your box get out of your box get out
and spread your winged arms
and fly before the cage's doors
truly shut and your plumage begins
to dim
because no facts you possess can convince
him or her or you or me or we or us
to believe something
they don't

the unwild american first world dream
is a needle in your vein
pumping you full of painkiller visions
of you him she he it they
divisions
and i'm so sick of not partaking
that i'm having withdrawals
night sweats nausea anxiety paranoia
brief glimpses into true fucking madness
and i've never been happier
one shitty situation or manager meeting

away
from saying fuck it all
giving away all my shit
and living the way the animals do

21st century caveman please let me be
that guy
on the corner
with a cup
or bowl
begging
people to buoy
him up because I think that's the last
place you'll ever
find god
in a place
like this
no, please, I don't want money sir
or madame, i've had enough of that
for a lifetime
just give me some bread and some calcium
and protein
and let me live
pity me, shame me, give me all of your hate
because I have nothing but love
and a bowl to be filled
with the stuff
of life.

-begging bowl-

Please come walk with me
a moment, or sit—here take this
cushion and sit with me while we talk.
This isn't really happening and that's okay.
We merely need a space
inside which exists
the possibility of happening.

You asked me about my bowl--
it sits in front of me or in my hands
always ready to accept offerings
from the universe.
Hand outs, favors, blessings--
all are accepted here.
Connotation no longer exists
when you accept anything
someone has to give.

I've always wanted to have nothing--
the desire sits and will continue to sit
as it does now
like a single, lit candle upstairs
in the corner of a darkened house--
an idea some say is stupid
and misguided and foolish
and does nothing productive
like the candle
for the rest of the house.

The flame persists and I wonder
about the galaxy of possibilities
found in following my feet
through wormholes of experience
I will never know
unless I go.

This me will be a different
one tomorrow either way,
but the possibility of becoming
a different new me
acts like sunlight refracting from glass
in the eyes of a crow.

I feel like it's in my blood.
My mother's brother ended up
walking the earth,
carrying the begging bowl
not quite a Buddha
and not quite like Kung Fu
but something wild,
untamed,
and resonating much more truly
with the rhythms of life.
We are the only animal
that pays to live.

I was a teenager when I met
two young men, no older than I am now--
they wandered along the beach
toward my friends and I
drawn by the fire we'd started.
They asked us if they could sit down.
They were from Minnesota,
the state where my father was born.
They'd been traveling cross country
and their van had broken down--
this was two months ago.
They'd been existing, buoyed up
by the kindness of strangers.
At the end of our time
I gave them the fifty dollars
my parents had given me
to spend how I liked.

All the pieces fit together.
Be nothing,
have nothing
I want to inspire myself
to the point where possible
and impossible are no longer words,
just sounds
that to the wild ear sound the same
differentiated by a single vibration.
Ignorance of phobic concepts
will deliver me,
buoyed upon the waves of all
that awakens awe.

-goonies never say die-

Back in the days
when I was still acid
drenched and believed
I was the Buddha
or a shaman
or whatever,
I visited that beach in Oregon
where they shot "The Goonies."
I tripped on two hits
with one of my best friends
and the girl
who was probably my soul mate.

Cannon Beach with the rocks
of behemoth proportions.
We walked down the beach
and let the acid
tickle its way up our spines.
We were smiling and laughing
and making long sighs
that sent shivers up and down
and flesh turns to braille.
Birds circled overhead,
over rocks
and the reality set in--
the birds actually
live there.

We the visitors left wet
impermanent
marks in the shape of feet
behind us as we frolicked
farther and farther
away
from the big, now small
rocks that stood in the water

crashing closer
as the tide came in.
The sun was beginning its descent
toward the horizon, downward,
throwing long shadows
and stretching our bodies
past the limit. Darkened
hyperbole
we were now giants
and magnets
to supernatural visions.

We dodged the icy inlets,
indicators of incoming tide,
leaping from bank to bank
as the grass on the dunes
bent under
weight of the wind.

And get this, everywhere we went
up and down the beach,
wherever we were,
we looked up,
and behold:
the clouds heavy, bulky were all
around--
except for where we stood.
A circular slice, cyllindrical
seemed carved clean
from the body of the clouds.
We glimpsed the now purple
blue of the sky,
felt for a fraction ephemeral,
effervescent, eternal, holy,
mystic.

-o, to be a cloud!-

The clouds are doing fun
things today--they're the kind
I like--cotton candying, aloft
and unreachable. Defined
edges, sunny around the sides,
bodies murky and full of grey.
A reflection of duality
inherent in all of life.

My twin told me that when
she dies, she wants to reincarnate
as a cloud. I can see why--
clouds are a reflection
of the Tao--all flows,
but none better than air--
it alights in places even water
can't reach.

Go with the flow
is the name of the game--
water is touched by rays
from the sun, drawn
upward effortlessly
forming into the heavenly
bodies that delight
us and conjure a playground
in our imaginations.
A rorschach test of the mind.

That one a dog, that one
a dragon. We delight in freedom
and the clouds reflect desire
for flight. Heavenly loftiness
that reawakens jealousy
toward birds.

So ineffable, the perception
of our eyes creates the cloud
into what it is.

The perfect perceivable object--
the cloud is whatever we need
it to be. Aspire to a level
like the cloud, for it is as
unattached
to our sight's result
as we ought to be
to the gaze of all.

-happening-

I like to watch things happen.
A happening
of a moment. Past, present,
and future blur
as something, anything
unfurls.

It feels like what gurus
and self help celebs
are always
going on about.
Be here now with me,
with the self
as time loses meaning,
increasing in value.

Stand in front of the painting,
and though it doesn't change,
watch closely
as you begin to bend.
It is not the art that moves,
it is you.

A droplet of ink in water,
watch it fall, splash,
dissipate: the black billowing
and blooming expansion
in real time.

The sun is coming up
over the hills
to the east,
sunlit tendrils reaching
farther and farther,
its grasp follows shortly

as our truest idol
shows itself,
is born,
gives us life,
Gives us light.

-my song-

I'm finding now
nothing beats the exhaustion
in having woken up
early and lived through
a day where I feel
purpose, and direction.
Pursuing the goals
I envision,
seeing grass
where before lay
desert. One step
at a time brings me closer
to where
to who
to what
I want to be.
No one else can do it for me.
I am grateful.

I make a list the night before,
say a prayer for protection
of those I love.
Everything within my control
I acknowledge and vow
to undertake
with my own hands.
The rest I surrender
to the universe,
like a butterfly
momentarily alighted
upon my palm.

Whether or not the future
will bring what I pray
for is not my concern.

I trust in the universe
to bring about the changes
that I can't bring myself.
Ours is a world
of energy, currents
upon currents,
amassing into a giant
technicolor stream.
Mine is but a current
within a current,
a ripple,
a whirling pool
of my intentions
surrounded
by everything else.

I will focus
on what is mine
and make it perfect,
or close to it: this
is how it must be,
because the universe
reflects
what I put in.
Dissatisfaction
and malcontent
only paralyze
and sow more seeds
of their ilk.
Gratitude is the song
I sing,
and the prayer
I speak.
Gratitude begets gratitude.
Before I know it,
I am holding a bouquet
of flowers
where a butterfly

once sat.
-august 2017, seattle wa-

-a beauty poem-

I want to talk about beauty--
no, not talk--
I want to show
you beauty,
make it felt
in the heart,
somewhere beyond the reach
of words.
Because words
are not
the thing itself--
words are fingers
pointing
toward the thing
itself.
They are the finger
pointing at the moon,
not the moon itself.

My mother used to collect
unicorns
because, she said,
they have mystique
and beauty.
She wasn't wrong,
and what's more,
she said it
simply.

Beauty strikes us in places
words can't reach.
A cloud
or a sunset
or a painting of them
is more

than the words we have
to name them
will ever be.

We recognize these things we see
not with words
but by the feelings
ignited within.
Electric stirrings inside
when I see a face I love
is reality, not the word, "face."

What then is ignited in us?
The same unknown spark
inside
that helps us
lift our arms,
dream our dreams,
and reach epiphanies--
the essence of all that is
is reflected
onto us.

We witness without what is within--
as above,
so below,
within,
without.

Cascading sequences of succulents,
spaces of emptiness
between
every
note,
the light at the end
of the tunnel.

All beauty begins

and ends
in harmony--
unity
borne
in unspoken recognition
that All
is One.

-the world breathes-

The world breathes.
The world sighs.

My chin rests on my windowsill,
window open. Eyes closed.

I hear the breathing of the world
and the sighing.

Is there any difference
between the two?

Is a sigh just a connotation
of breathing?

Maybe I hear a sigh
because of the heaviness

in my body, in my mind.
These feelings change

like the weather. Wind whistles
through the branches and the leaves.

Do I hear the breathing of wind through
or is it friction of leaves on leaves?

How to determine answers
to questions like these...

Roaring sighs or breaths from cars
doppler toward me,

growing loud to a crescendo,
then doppler away, quieting

as if they'd never been
at all.

The world inhales to exhale
just like me.

Maybe unity is found in this:
the unmistakable sound

of life.

-shinrin yoku-

A Japanese phrase
that means, "to bathe
in a forest."
I know where to go
to perform
this ritual
to renew
the eternal
within.
Do you?

I drive down 25th
until it turns into 23rd,
past stadium
and then left
right after I cross 520.
Wind down toward
the arboretum,
ditch the car
and my anxiety.
Skip into the cathedral
of conifers.

U-Dub Arboretum.
My forest bathtub.
The eternal breath sounds
high in the trees.
Brings my own breath
forward.
Not until now
do I realize
how trapped it was
before.

I move at any pace

my feet decide.
No one bothers me.
Branches bob in the wind,
leaves evergreen wave between
spaces of limbs.
My lids close over my eyes.
Remembering lost languages
supplanted by my modernity,
I hear the voice
of the world
spoken through tree tongues.

They tell me everything
is okay
without saying.

My breaths come slower
and easier.
My shoulders soften
and the corners
of my mouth
lift.

-mud season-

Almost mud season.
They say Seattle has eleven seasons--
it's third winter
now and then comes mud season.
And I feel it coming.
Wind cuts through clothing.
Earth is soft under my steps,
clinging to the cleats of boots.
My soul grasped for growth
these last cold months.
I've done a bit. Not
as much as I wanted.
Others say they can see it--
always so hard to see
ourselves. Mirrors don't do justice
to our hopes or fears. The most
it helps is for me to fix this cowlick.
Try to remember
I am perfect as I am
except for when I'm not.
Winter still clinging,
speaking through my teeth.
But spring's fingers are always groping
through that dark, weary season.
Days grow longer.
Light returns to evening,
spring gains a hold. Sunrays sink
into skin and spark the seed
of the soul and suddenly
smiles aren't so hard to swing.
Effervescence of seeds sprouting
inside awaken.
It's become effortless.
Mud season is here.
The lotus is blooming.

No mud, no lotus.
-march 2018, seattle wa-

-shedding a skin-

Shedding an old skin
worn for too long.
An itchy and scary
process. The new
skin is sensitive
to light and touch.

There is more to life
than who I had become. Fear
is a cozy blanket
until it threatens
to strangle and even
then, the effort
required for freedom
frightens in a different way.

The devil you know
is supposed to be better
than the devil you don't.
Nothing is scarier
than effort to those of us
who have engrained
poison into our habits.
Insanity, the repetition
of what hasn't worked
was my daily prescription.

Now. Now. Now.
I want it all now
and if it doesn't work
at first, then throw it all
away. Fuck whatever
moves, take the pill
that's offered—up
or down it doesn't really

matter because I'm not here
to get high, I'm here
to forget that I am God.

The morning comes
and finds me
unchanged. I'm almost
thirty. Nothing has worked
so far. My soul knows
what is needed--
my brain resists
and says that it's impossible.

It's only impossible
until anything is better
than being who I was
yesterday. Realizing
I am love, and I deserve
what I've always tried
to give to others,
I direct it back at myself.

Flowers bloom within
and without. I am leaning
toward the sun. Petals
sprout and spread wide
open. Each new task
of love I undertake
on behalf of myself
is another ray
of light to grow
this garden and dry
the sleeve of skin
so that I may burst
forth, renewed--
reborn.

-alchemy mask-

The pair of shoes hanging
by its laces from the power
line at the end of my block
is gone. Unsure
of when they left I'm left
to make my own mirror
of when it happened.

Often-nodded symbol
of my profession
of three years, they shone
an affirmation
of my doings,
of my sellings.
They pointed to me,
and I to them:
this place is where that
sort of thing goes on.

I'm not ashamed to admit
it was what I did,
except to my mother.
I'm not sure what she would say.
Hopefully she realizes
it's only part, not the end
of the story.
I did what I wanted
when I wanted
a handful of years
and I'd never tasted
such freedom.
Freedom is what we risk
in a game like this.

My name was known

places I didn't want it
thrown. Amidst this,
I realized I am
not that. I expressed a wish
to be something else
and take on new skin.

Adding is greater
than subtracting from the world.
Energetic equation
equals transformation—real life
alchemy here as my face
became someone else's.

Some time after, I noticed
that the shoes
and their strings
vanished from the line.

-a new leaf-

There is a plaintive perfection
in the falling of a leaf--
orange maple a sprawling
hand, spinning, it almost
floats
downward,
a lesson
of graceful surrender
to gravity
the eternal force.

There are lessons
learned from trees.
Possibly the oldest
of all the souls.
I figure if I want to be one
some day,
observation is key.

Each year as autumn creeps
close, the nights grow
longer—a shut down
signal to the trees.
The plant grows dormant
until the days grow bright
and the process backflips--
buds return to branches.

Do trees worry
about what they look
like when their leaves
have fallen, bark bones
standing stark against
the grey curtain of sky?

The days are growing
shorter. But I'm beginning
to see better than ever.
Anxiety, night terrors, sleep
paralysis were already
within me, and here they prepare
me for what I will be.
Leaves leaving my frame, foundation
exposed among the elements,
to the scrutiny
of the world.
Leaves fertilize my roots
as I grow with time.

I delve within myself,
search for the rays
of the occluded
sun remaining seeded
in my soul. As the work
is done and my soul embarks
on a mission to love
itself,
days will lengthen,
nights grow short

and branches will bend with weight
of blessed fruit.

-making a mountain-

Mole hills are mountains
from an ant's perspective,
or the person looking the other
way right before he trips.
Mountains can be mole hills
to a god, or someone flying
overhead in an airplane.
There are mountains within mountains.
We do not try to conquer
Everest on our first ever climb.
We climb mole hills
before challenging that mountain.

When things seem too overwhelming,
simplify.
My moms quote in her senior yearbook
was "keep it simple, stupid."
Take it from "things"
to "thing."
Work in the order of operations.
What is needed most must be done
first. And everything after flows
with the momentum
of your efforts.

Each mountain starts
as a molehill,
As will the mountain
of your accomplishments.
Even if you don't see results
after one day
resist the urge
to say it's "only" something.

"Only" is your first step

to everything. A journey
is made from single steps
and the destination
has never been the goal.
The journey is everything.
Take your time in every
and all things that you do.
One day you will stand
on top of your very own
mountain.

-the two thumbed hand-

I've always wanted it tattooed
somewhere on my body.
I can never decide where.
Any place is a good place
I guess,
especially since almost all of it
is free territory.
All the same I want it somewhere
giving the impact it holds
for me. Where is the best spot
to place protection from the evil eye?

A symbol of protection
in all faiths--
a representation of a father's arms
and a mother's love,
two things we're forever seeking
when we become orphans.
Hamsa, hamsa, hamsa,
tfu, tfu, tfu—please spare me that
bad luck
and may my parents live a hundred years
of youth.

The word means "five"
and "five fingers of the hand"--
one of my friends did a reading
to determine my life path's number
by combining the letters of my name
and the date of my birth.
The number I drew turned out to be
five--
I don't believe in coincidence.
Khamsa says that I am
a spirit of change, creative

manifestation of form,
magic maker.

To guard against the evil eye,
raise your right hand, fingers
slightly apart—a counter
curse meant to blind
the aggressor.
Or utter the phrase "khamsa
wa-khamis" which means,
"five" and "Thursday"--
Thursday is today, the fifth
day of the week, long known
to be a day for magic rites
and pilgrimages to the tombs
of our most revered saints
to rid us of the effects
of the evil eye.

I write this poem on Thursday,
the Winter Solstice,
and the alignment of all
strikes me between the eyes.
I have a friend
who once placed an enchantment
of protection over me
and I aim to do the same
with the magic in these lines
for all who read.
It is the darkest day of the year
but not for me.

Know you are protected, love of mine--
fear no thing
and no thing will fear you.
Press your palm to mine
and let us see each other's sight,
eye to eye.

After tonight
we begin the quest
to watch the growth
of summer's light.

-stargazer-

Petals reaching upward
and outward, toward
the four directions.
On the edges white
like sacred sheets
on lovers' beds,
seeping pinker
into the center
and at its heart,
indigo.

The night I met the woman
who was probably my soul mate--
she followed me up spiral
staircase to my bedroom.
I guessed the flower
she wanted at her wedding
and after our clothes
were shed, I glimpsed
the same flower etched
on her ribcage. We had met
before.

And after, months or maybe
a year, she filled the flower
in. She jumped and giggled
each time the needle
buzzed against her bones.
The artist told her
not to move—her eyes
leaked stars from their edges,
the touch of her hands against
mine.

One sixth of my life spent

with another lover
of white and pink petals
and me, for whatever reason
I hadn't yet discovered.
I exhausted options
to display my insides--
it was always there,
an eternal sigil
emblazoned
on my banner of
love.

Now I am alone.
Not quite lonely--
the past has its place
It has placed me here
where I spin the future
in my hands.
Right now I envision
the same pouring petals
and pistils and the sigil
unstained remains
in my sight—high pitched, lily,
perfect.

-lunatic-

It's a new moon
and I'm acting
accordingly. Yesterday
I let go of all the anchors
that weren't keeping
me grounded. Thoughts
and guilts had begun
to curdle and stunt my growth.

The moon has power,
whether you acknowledge
it or not. It moves the tides
and plants seeds of emotion
we are meant to grow.
It's a new moon
and I'm here dreaming
about what will come.
Living with intention
is my new resolution.

I feel like the moon--
at different moments
I look like someone
else, and sometimes
I'm not seen at all.
But those in tune
still feel my gravity's
pull. I will try to live
my life by the schedule
of the moon. A place
and time for all
selves and guises.

New moon is now
and it's the same for new

beginnings. I give power
to the moon by following
her direction. Tonight
I dream the dreams
that I will be able to touch
by the time the moon is full.
And when the moon is full
I will reflect on the patterns
of action and thought
that delivered me here.

Through practice I will forge
reality from what skeptics
call myths. The magic
of past generations will revive
under the efforts of this modern
mystic. Not much of a witch,
but I'm getting better as a poet.
Much more digital in my delivery
these days, but the spells
I cast with these words are
analog as ever.
-october 2017, enumclaw wa-

- chill with Bob Ross-

People say TV rots your brain,
but I think they forgot about Bob Ross.
Watching his stuff on Netflix calms
me down. Life lessons abound
in the sotto tones of this dude's voice.
Standing there in front of his easel,
in his denim jeans and button up
shirt, eternal trademark afro.
Poster child of chill,
Zen master as fuck.
He used to be a drill sergeant, did you know?
Then he stopped and decided
not to yell again. He might be the best
example of a human I can point
to in steering myself toward a true
North. "You have absolute power
here," he says. And I'm not sure
if he's talking about art or life.
Maybe they're the same thing.
"You can make it whatever
you want it to be." Again,
is this real life? He paints
a mountain in two strokes
of the brush. My mind is blown.
"You're going to have to make
some choices now," he says,
Again seemingly speaking more
than he knows. A tuning fork
goes off within as I watch,
because I know how right he is.
How will I know what's right
and what's not? So much riding
on this, so much responsibility
for someone who just recently
started cooking for himself.

"Each painting is as individual
as people. You paint the kind
of world you see
and that's the kind that's right."
Why didn't I see this as a child,
I wonder, as the wonder of his words
wander through my mind--the way
I see the world is the way it is.
The way you see it
is the way it is. Kaleidoscopic
quilting, stitches of perspective
composing what is. Possibilities
only as limited
as we make them.

-remote control-

We all have our own gravity.
We attract what we attract.
Energy, mercurial
concept, constantly flowing,
unchanging in its very being,
which is in itself the definition
of change. I have never been good
at accepting change. Not quite
all my fault. Human nature craves
the feeling of control. Why is the phrase
"What's going on?" so terrifying?

I have plans to get a tattoo
on my chest that reads, "NO CONTROL"
with some other dope shit
along with it. I crave control
yet my higher self knows
the illusion. We play
at the smaller game
and try to win it
in order to forget the bigger,
cosmic game,
which can never be won,
only played.

Life is motion
in the same way
life is change.
If you want to know how
to imbibe the energy
of the universe,
keep moving.
The pulsing of the universe
reflects experience and what
we call "the present. The time

is now
and it should never be wasted,
especially when looking
for energy. Control is a lie
but it's not a fact to say
that we control nothing.
We control what we control
by paying attention
and being present
and doing what we can
to raise ourselves up
and pay attention
on the ride of life.

Stillness is also a part of life
and a key ingredient to energy.
If you want to create ripples
in reality and impress yourself
upon the world,
be still. The law of attraction
dwells in these words.
To know what you want
is half of this battle,
and the other half
is focusing your intent.
Knowing what you want
is a wish you speak
to the great Magnet.
Focusing your intent
is an agreement
made with yourself.
When these occur,
the great Magnet
and yourself
resonate...frequencies match
and being present
delivers what you seek.

Seeking without seeking,
such a paradox,
but isn't that like life?
Know what you seek.
Do not move toward it.
Move along the path
that makes you better
and your treasure
will be delivered
to you.
-august 2017, seattle wa-

-what we need-

the other day a friend told me
my poems sound like a front bottoms
song. then, another day a different friend
played me some of their songs
and i liked what i heard.
because no one needs poems
with arcane words
and elevated speech
anymore. we're not trying to talk
to people who read this stuff--
we're talking to kids on twitter
and facebook to bring them back
from where they're dwelling,
forgetting decency because
being a dick is so much harder
in person. i want poetry
with dirt under its nails,
and a filthy fucking mouth.
i'm talking "fucks" "shits" and
"blow me's"--desperate
first thought-best thought
phrases and speakers
who wear their souls on their
faces.
art, believe it or not, is not about
being smart. art is about whatever
the fuck i'm feeling and please
please tell me that you've felt it too.
because otherwise i'm alone here
just like i always feared.
you have permission to feel
whatever you're feeling at any given
time, and you didn't need it from me
in the first place.
and don't believe for a second

you're the only one who's felt this way--
you are not alone and seek these lines out
if you ever feel like that again.
then one day sit down
or stand up and open your notebook
or grab a napkin or use your computer
or your trusty fucking cell phone
and tell me exactly how you feel--
and when you've done all that
be brave and show it to your friends.
it will scare you and surprise most of them,
but i promise you that no price is too high
to pay for journeying back to yourself.

-you are yours, i am mine-

I used to think I wanted
to be someone's everything,
their moon
their stars
and the energy
holding it all together.

So much responsibility,
the heaviness of those
words, "I want you
forever." The words clank
like chains, binding you
there, while all around,
everything changes.

For the first time in my life
my head seems to be screwed
on right. Mental health
is job one,
Physical health right behind.
How to do this without losing
balance?

We are fighting a war of the psyche
and of the heart, and losing
so far. From all corners
advertisements, and other people
selling shit, trying to get us to buy
in to the idea that we're nothing
without someone else.

Hallmark, TV, even the music
on the radio, yelling at us
in all capital letters, BUY THIS,
GET THAT, AND NEVER LOOK WITHIN

FOR THE ANSWERS TO YOUR QUESTIONS.

Obsession and possession
are deemed to be the thing
we should be after.
Oh, to have a person
who wants me
and only me.
Sweet dreams are made of these,
who are we to disagree?
Life has always been a dream,
but we're sharing it with everyone
else: whose wishes take precedence
here, where all is possible
but nothing stays the same?

The only truth is this: you are the only
person you will ever have for good.
So protect that person and treat
them right. Everyone else goes away
in the end. But you are here
and life exists,
only for you.

-me to me-

Be the sun, be the sun, be the sun,
I tell myself.
There are others
who need your words,
need your vibes.
You're nowhere
near done yet.
One day at a time.
Fake it
til you make it.

Remember, remember, remember:
blessings are every day.
Bless those who are in darkness.
Light is in their future.
And bless those who are in light.
Darkness is past
and future.
Shadows are made by light.
Both are in all.

Shine your light, your light, your light
to soak up the dew.
Spring is coming.
Soon enough
you won't have to try
so hard
to shake the dust
from your wings.
Days are getting longer.
You know you'll trade
an extra hour
of sleep
for that.

Clouds build from the rising water
touched by fingers
of the sun.
Could it be that each ray
you give
builds
another cloud
for yourself?
If it were true,
would you do it different
at all?

It's a cycle, it's a cycle, it's a cycle.
Never static, always
morphing
into something new.
Everything moves according
to the great magnet.
And though they don't want to admit,
you are at the center
of the wheel. Everything
moves according to you.

You know the truth of this,
resounding
in the golden seed
within.
If you weren't here
you would not be witness
to this ocean
of dreams.
The world would be lacking
and for you, it would
not turn.
You know
you would do it
just the same.

-i see stars-

"I know nothing but the sight
of the stars makes
me dream." Van Gogh wrote
that in a letter to his brother.
An artist as talented
as that also wrote
beautiful words.

Seeing with your own eyes
instead of someone else's--
the ultimate goal, it seems--
and the way to make this world
yours. Van Gogh wanted to be
a missionary before he found
art. He started out wishing
to do God's work
and ended up creating
fractals, snippets of the face
of God. He brought us
a sense of God no one
knew existed.

I always looked for God
in every place I could think,
except inside myself.
Now that I've looked
there, I feel like I've finally
touched him. I only pray
I can show you
something even half
as bright
as what
has inspired
me.
-august 12 2017, salmo river ranch bc-

-eye contact-

I've experienced the dawning
familiarity
between
two souls
when they realize
they are one.
In a mass of people
I have found you.
A tuning fork in my soul,
when our gazes collide.
A reflection in
your eyes
of my soul.
and we are one.

-angel #1-

People paint you closest
to Satan but I know
what's in your heart--
a love of the sound
of flowers that rings
in your head
and the tears that fall
from your eyes
when you hear the strains
of something classical
with no words.
They are cheap things
anyway but they're the closest
I have to pouring out
my soul to show you
what I mean.
Your halo is made of hairlessness
of your crown, like a monk,
and the black hat
you're sometimes known to wear.
You show your wings
in the never speaking behind
my eyes. I know your intent
from sharing so much.

Eyes of others and mouths
they lie. I know
the truth of your being--
you love and seek love
always.

-angel #2-

Your real name is the name
of my mother, and the name
you go by is my favorite
animal, which is my mother's
favorite, too.

The ink on your skin
is etched in my insides,
colors and flowers
I would love to ring in my ears.
Words indelible
in my brain and symbols
of alchemy, transmutation
of the self assisted
by you in me so much
I'm become someone else.
You forced nothing
yet here I am to sing
your praise.
I will always love you
and how we both
understand before we speak.
Your halo keeps changing
colors and I love each one
like it's new
and I'm seeing you again
for the first time.

I have lines and lines
more for you,
I give them all
for free
because no reward
is better than the taste
of singing your praise.

O sing in me, O muse,
give me gilded lily
tongue to ramble on
until you're in my arms
or not.

-to bukowski-

Bukowski,
I wish I could be like you.
But maybe my parents loved me
more than yours
loved you.
Or at least showed it
more than yours.

You are
how you are
because of how
your old man
was.
Just like I am
how I am
because of how my
old man is.

Maybe it's because
I see the world
as more
beautiful
than it is
that I'm like me
instead of being
like you.

I know you still cared
but the way you did it
could have fooled
almost
anyone.

More than anything
else

I value
your honesty.

More than anything
else
I want
to be that.

I love that you write
about cats--
I was reading
one of your books
with my cat
on my lap.
I scratched
his cheeks
and he drooled
on the pages.
I chuckled and teased
him, then he sneezed
and sprayed
spittle
everywhere.
I roared
and he leaped
from my lap
to some place
with less noise.

I understand
this
and I know
you would too.

-what does an artist see?-

I'm so glad you asked,
my friend.
I step out from my car
and walk around.
The lawn is frosted over,
temperature below zero.
My brain doesn't say this:
instead it speaks through
filter and sees glittered
granules of condensation, reminder
from the fairies. It is still winter.

I step through the parking lot
after a day of rain. Sunlight
spreads itself. In a puddle
oil slicks are present.
In here, iridescence ribboning
across the expanse of liquid
mirror, painting this face,
that sky a pattern rarely
found in nature.
Images of oceans polluted
may come to mind. In here,
right now, there is beauty
in the sickness. Strength born
from struggle.

A discussion within.
Images present themselves.
We surge to inter them
into boxes. Burial behind our eyes,
surrendering meaning
in favor of definition.
Artists are not born.
They are made.

Lenses lent by learned language
blind us from what we perceive,
put a eyeful of easy entries
into the fields we create
with our questions.
New answers need new questions.
New eyes need new answers.
Stop asking what this is.
Instead ask,
what could this be?

-the fly will come to you-

I've been doing this thing
for a year and a half.
It's humbling
and exciting
to know that the best poems
I'm going to write
haven't been written.
A comfort to know
the more you do something
the better you get.

What will I write about
years from now?
I hope no more poems
about how I wish
everyone was more like me.
And by that I mean:
I wish more people held the door
for people. Let other people
into their lane. Left bigger tips.
Realized the futility of fighting
for what they want.
There is no salvation in holy wars
or trying to make wars
holy.

More poems about nature,
please...I'll tell you
what the people want.
They want something sacred.
More poems about God,
with a small "g"
if you like--
and how he is you
and me

and us,
the sum
of all our parts.

Poems about my children
or why I chose not to have them.
Poems about the children
of my friends and what it's like
to be a fun uncle
and see the world
experienced
through the eyes of a child.
Poems about family
and what I've found it to mean.

I will let them come to me,
these poems.
Writing them for me
is my holy war.
It is my sacred. And to win
the war, I must not fight.
Patience is a virtue
for a reason.
The frog in the pond
and the venus flytrap
are my metaphors
here. Do not seek the fly--
it will come to you.

-see abundance and there will be abundance-

See abundance and there will be
abundance. Seeing is not believing,
believing is Seeing. If we were to wait
for the abundance to show itself
we would wait a lifetime.
Yet the signs are all around
if we choose to look.

I told a friend yesterday that I don't
have money for food. She invited
me over and made me dinner,
and sent me home with a bag
filled with food. The story doesn't end
there--later that night I visited
someone else and mentioned
my friend's gift. She offered me
some of her food.

I feel like I knew this would happen
before I was shown proof.
What possessed me to tell that friend
about my situation?
I knew the result because I felt
help would be given
if I were to ask.
Life is a feeling process
and by feeling our way
we seem to find our path.

The signs are all around us,
we can create magic
with our thoughts.
Know that there is enough
to provide for all. Chaplin
said, "The good earth is rich

and can provide for everyone."
And he was right. There is enough
to provide for everyone.
People are willing to help
if you are willing to ask.
-july 2017, seattle wa-

-princess-

The cat comes upstairs to my room
in the attic every night.
He hops on my bed
and walks to me,
always looking me
in the eye. If my phone is in my hand
he'll bump my hands
with his face. If I'm typing
on my laptop, he'll lay down
on top of my wrists. If I'm laying
down, he'll walk onto my chest,
bump the cool end of his nose
against my cheek. Sometimes
when I don't pet him
he'll reach up and put the pads
of his paws against my face.

I take my hands and put them
on his cheeks.
The movement of my hands
is very subtle—somewhere
between a scratch, a rub,
and a massage—
as my fingers move,
his eyes shutter
closed
and a noise vibrates from somewhere
between his chest and his throat.
I rub hardest right where I imagine
his cheek muscles to be--
the vibrations increase.
Scratching over his eyebrows
and behind his ears
works too. At some point
I brush my face

into the feather fur
underneath his chin. His purr continues
and I'm moved
to tell him
I love him.

And then at some point I come back up
from the softness
and the smell of his fur,
which remind me of earth
and air,
and he looks up into me.
Yellow eyes and black pupils
that widen
as our eyes meet.
Neither of us breaks the contact
of our eyes.
Still we look.
I lose track of time.

-snow, angel-

It's snowing.
Just look at the streetlight--
just there.

Pinprick motes of frozen water
filter downward
and pile up.

It's finally grown dark
so I'm opening my presents
like I did when I was young.

Noise is muffled,
no sound escapes.
I exist within a snowglobe.

Wonder piles on wonder:
It's never snowed on Christmas
here for me before.

There is a certain magic
in the way time works
toward moments like this.

Last year I wanted to die
and rain was all I got--
Now I'm changed

and suddenly the world
is brand new,
unmarked like the powder

falling for me and you.
Witness the divine
timing of fate.

I may go make an angel,
but not just yet.
Let me revel here for now.

-memory poem-

My room, minefield of memories.
Emotion engrained in each explosive
possession. I would love to give
this all away, strike out
on my own, nothing
but a bag and my bag
of bones, myself. But every property
piece holds a story
I love to tell
sometimes more than once
to whoever will listen.
I fear that I'm becoming my elders--
tattoos of security,
safety belts
only real
until death.
My hands already palsy, shaking
like my grandpa's when he eats soup.

Steady hand absent—no confidence
to abandon ship, be borne
up on mirage-colored waves,
universal energy that responds
to exhibitions of faith.
Losing my faith like my grandpa
losing his mind. He accused
my dad of stealing from him and worries
loudly about the big black boyfriend
he imagines my grandma has.
Ugly shadow self descent
into madness. The real thing
is not so romantic.
In it we lose our memories,
substitute our fears
in the erosion of memory.

Occurring
little by little,
identity so fragile,
like a strand of floss,
running between too tightly packed
teeth.

Is this living to old age
or dying?

Fast forward some decades--
I wake up in a room,
trappings I've unrecognized
on walls whose color I might remember--
like waking from a dream
in someone else's house.
But the dawn of recognition
doesn't come,
no sigh of relief,
and I'm alone
here where memory abandoned
me.

-may 20 2018, seattle wa-

-year of the dragon-

Finally moving into my power
accepting that I was born
in an auspicious year.
I'm here for you, for me,
for your children and theirs
and seven generations and more
onward. Change is coming.
If I'm not taking part
I should get out of the way.

The number one--
new beginnings. The number
of will power and ambition,
taking the lead and most of all,
love.
Everything is here because
of us. The experience is not
experienced without you
and your presence. The sky
is not a ceiling.
Beyond sky is more sky--
but we call it space.
Infinity abounds.

Once at a festival I was asked
my birthdate. So I told him--
Oh, a Gemini dragon,
he said, and thought. Then,
that makes sense
why you're not intimidated
by me. Apparently
he was foreboding—a darkened
Scorpio, but to me another
soul, reflection of me.
I'm not sure if I'd ever been cowed

before—but never since.

The number nine--
philanthropy, to love
one's fellow man
who is really no one else
but you, but me.
Selflessness and charity,
purpose of the soul.
We are here for we,
vibration of understanding
Say it with me: "Niiiiiiine."
Similar to "OM"--
sound that created the universe.
We are that and resonate
the manifestation
of its vibration.

John Lennon's magic number
was nine and so is mine.
I might have taken it from him
but I've made it my own.
All you need is love,
what a line. Peace be with you
my brother, my sister
because we cannot create anew
with malicious intent.
Cast off the chains of past
and transcend your habits
with me as we leave behind
a world of reaction and move
forward into action.

The number eight--
the number of infinity,
reappearance of ever expanding
space. There is no end
but a new beginning.

Giving and receiving
are one and the same.
I give to you, I give to me.
Scarcity is propaganda--
there is enough for all
because the good earth
provides for those who give
thanks and steward the land
into future hands.

I was born in the year of the dragon.
A mythical symbol to live up to.
My year of birth denotes
me as a dragon of earth,
smart, ambitious, and hard
working. I only really agree
with the first. Ancient times
told that dragons could control
all the world.
I'm not sure I want all that--
but my world is thirsting
for change. Constant
but who will direct its flow?
I'm not scared
of what anyone thinks.
I left my fear
in my other pants.
Besides, dragons don't wear pants.

A second eight to round it off--
an ouroboros, a snake
or dragon, eating its own tail.
Symbol of infinity.
Gemini dragon has two heads.
Watch the past, watch the future--
at the center the present is ours.
Every moment there's a choice.
What will you choose?

I've made my decision.
Presence, presents, gifts, gives.
Infinity is us, infinity is ours.

-june 9, 2018-

Today is my birthday
and it's also apparently
best friends day.
Taking stock of life
and its changes
when you become
your own best friend.
It was spitting rain
last night when I turned
30, but by noon the sun
was out, with cracks
of blue between fluffy
limbs of clouds building
cumulously in the sky
like they were doing it
on purpose
for me,
my eyes gifted a present
I could thank no one
besides myself
and the world for--
for making it here
long enough to behold
and for being here
before, after, but especially
now to be beheld.
Who makes a life happen?
No hands clear a path
for another. Hands belong
to someone who clears
the way.
-june 9 2018, seattle wa-

-welcome home-

How long has it been
since you felt at home?

I hear voices
of a theme--
repeated visions of souls
adrift in sea of confusion
casting looks for a sign
their sails are pointed right.

"Home," a two-sided coin—
one side of home
a dwelling place,
where life is lived. The second
face of the word the end point
of a journey--
a destination.
Confusion crops to surface
tagging two targets
at once.

Confusion compounds
when the seeker
seeks approval
in his seeking from any
eyes other than his own--
how can one approve the ways
in which another seeks?
Our world, greater dream,
seeks to convince us
of the reality of illusions
dancing before us, appearing
as solids, but in truth
nothing but vibration.

Advertisements and affirmations

from all corners
echo we will never
be enough
unless we buy this
or do that,
always relying on our sight
and its tendency to look
around rather than
within.

The only home you need
is not the one
you have to mortgage
or the one you left
when you were young.
It's the one you lived in
since the day you were born.
Your breaths built the house
whose foundations are your bones.
Your vessel
in this ocean of confusion
is also
your compass.

The weather vane within
will whisper
the wind's direction
and point you proper
to your true north.
The ocean you find inside
will be dark
but it will be warm,
not unlike the womb
from which you came--
imbued with
a strange orange glow.

Quiet the noisy assault

on your senses--

close your eyes and tell yourself,
"Welcome home."

Made in the USA
Columbia, SC
19 May 2019